Hungry Halloween

featuring

Movie Monster Munchies, Bewitched Buffet, and Dead Man's Diner

by
Beth Jackson Klosterboer

Food Styling
and
Photography by
Beth Jackson Klosterboer

Drawings by
Ekaterina Selivanova

Edited by
Cheri Burns

Hungry Halloween
featuring Movie Monster Munchies, Bewitched Buffet, and Dead Man's Diner
is an original publication by Candy Garden Publishing.

For information contact:
Beth Jackson Klosterboer at
Beth@HungryHalloween.com

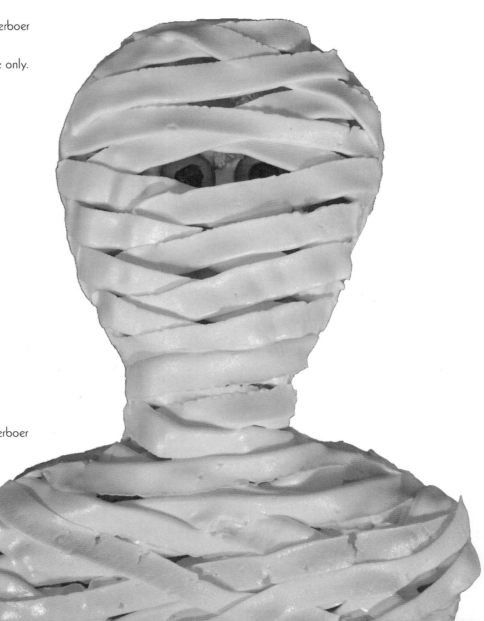

Photography © 2010 Beth Jackson Klosterboer

Drawings © 2010 Ekaterina Selivanova

Edited by: Cheri Burns

First edition June 2010

TABLE OF CONTENTS

INTRODUCTION 5

SPECIAL THANKS TO:

My husband, Jim, for all your advice and encouragement. I couldn't have created this book without your love and support. Thanks for sharing your enthusiasm and for helping me plan and host our over the top Halloween parties. I appreciate all of the hours you have spent building sets, creating props, and brainstorming ideas.

My daughter, Katya, for your amazing artwork. I'm so grateful to have you in my life and to have your artwork in my book.

My friend, Cheri, for your wonderful creativity and painstaking editing work.

My parents, Louise and Ken, for always encouraging me to pursue my creative ventures and helping me achieve my goals.

My sister, Kathy, for the endless hours in the candy kitchen and for your incredible support and friendship.

My brother, Kevin, and niece, Kayleigh, for filming and photographing our parties.

To the other members of my family for always supporting my culinary endeavors: Gregg, Martha, Jeff, Amanda, Brian, Sandy, April, Kenny, Katy, and Sam.

My friend, Kim, for your enthusiasm and countless hours of help in the kitchen. I'm glad we're both nuts about parties.

To all of my family and friends who have attended my parties and inspired me to create this book, especially those who have helped with the decorating, cooking, cleaning, organizing, and filming at the events.

Judi, Odesa, Holly,
Bev, Catherine, Christine, Angela,
Hannah, Christy,
Kathleen, Brooke, Emily,
Lizzie, Cameron, Olivia,
John, Vanessa,
Don, Trent, and Vickie

INTRODUCTION

Once a year we gather together dressed in elaborate costumes to celebrate the most ghoulish of holidays. Halloween parties have become increasingly popular, as those of us who enjoyed the frivolity of a night spent begging for candy dressed as a bed sheet ghost look to recapture the fun of our youth.

Whether you are looking to host an elaborate Halloween bash or are simply in search of a fun treat to serve your kids on Beggars' Night, *Hungry Halloween* is a great resource filled with delicious and imaginative recipes.

Each October my husband and I host several hair-raising Halloween parties. Having worked as an event planner, I know what it takes to throw a successful party, so we go all out. We choose a theme and plan everything to coordinate with that theme, including the menu.

Food is such an integral part of any holiday celebration and clever food can elevate a Halloween party to new heights. Over the years I've developed really unique recipes for our parties and my party guests have encouraged me to create a collection of these fun ideas and share them with other Halloween party hosts.

I've divided this book into three chapters, each with its own unique party theme. Each chapter includes a wide array of Halloween recipes as well as a few Halloween decorating ideas.

Frankenstein's monster, vampires, mummies, and werewolves come to life in **Movie Monster Munchies**. Serve your guests Vampire Chips with Blood Fondue, Werewolf Won Tons, Cheesy Franken-heads, and Creepy Crepes. To complete the theme, you can turn your house into a movie theater complete with a concession stand, movie screen, and ticket booth.

Witches, black cats, cauldrons, spiders, and even rats magically transform into delectable food in **Bewitched Buffet**. Impress everyone when you serve Cackling Crackers with Full Moon Dip along with Beefy Broomsticks and Black Widow Bites. See how you can make your home look like a witch's lair filled with spell books and potions.

Create a Fifties style diner with a gory twist and host a **Dead Man's Diner** party. Transform your kitchen into a diner filled with severed body parts and dress up in classic waitress uniforms to serve up Hand-Burgers, Bloody Finger Fries, Bone Chips and Open Face Sandwiches.

I hope you enjoy making many of these fun recipes for your next Halloween event. To find more recipes and party planning tips, go to my website: **http://www.HungryHalloween.com/**.

Happy Halloween!

MOVIE MONSTER MUNCHIES DECOR IDEAS

Transform your kitchen into a movie theater concession stand by decorating your counter-tops with popcorn buckets and movie theater candy boxes. Purchase or make a concessions sign and add movie theater images to complete the look.

Decorate a room or basement to look like the lobby of a movie theater. Print a big sign displaying the name of your cinema and post it at the lobby entrance. Hang classic monster movie posters on the walls and add spider webs and spiders. Build a ticket booth out of cardboard and sheets of clear acetate and add zombies or skeletons dressed in classic ticket taker uniforms. Illuminate the dark room using black light to bring out all the spooky details.

Cover your windows with black curtains and add an eerie glow to the room by putting orange light bulbs in your lamps. Decorate with movie monster cardboard standees (available on-line).

Design a laboratory using a store bought mad scientist and plastic wall hangings. Create a monster by adding plastic hands and head to an old suit filled with pillows.

MOVIE MONSTER MUNCHIES

Halloween is a time when
we revel in being frightened.
We may shudder,
but we can't help but take a peek
at the monsters under our bed.
These monsters come alive in our
nightmares and in the movies.

Classic horror movies are filled
with scary characters including
blood sucking vampires,
flesh hungry werewolves,
undead mummies,
and eight feet tall monsters.

Set the stage for
these classic movie monsters
to come to life
by serving
Aaa-rrrr-ooolive Bread,
Dreamy Draculas,
Crispy Frankie Pops
and
Mummy Lasagna
at your monster movie
themed party.
Compliment these yummy dishes
with concession stand favorites
like popcorn, nachos, and candy.

PORTRAIT OF A MONSTER

You don't need to be an artist to create this delicious masterpiece.
A layer of artichoke dip creates a simple background. Green spinach dip is piped over the background to create the monster's face and crushed blue corn tortilla chips are sprinkled on to create all the gory details.

Ingredients:

Artichoke Dip Layer:
2 (14 oz) jars marinated artichokes
5 cloves roasted garlic*
6 ounces cream cheese, softened
1/2 cup mayonnaise
1 cup freshly grated Parmesan cheese

Spinach Dip Layer:
10 ounces frozen spinach, thawed
1 can water chestnuts
2 ounces cream cheese, softened
3/4 cup sour cream
1/2 cup mayonnaise
2 tablespoons grated Parmesan cheese
5 cloves roasted garlic*
1/2 teaspoon salt
1/2 teaspoon lemon juice
1/2 teaspoon onion powder
2 ounces blue tortilla chips

Special Equipment Needed:
Monster Template (page 97)
1 clear stencil sheet
Hobby knife
Food processor
Pastry brush
Disposable pastry bag (or zip top bag)

To Create Monster Stencil: Copy the Monster Template (page 97), increasing the size to fit an 8 1/2" x 11" page. Set copy on a cutting board and lay clear stencil sheet on top. Use a hobby knife to cut out the black areas of the image.

Drain artichokes. Pour artichokes, roasted garlic cloves, cream cheese, mayonnaise, and Parmesan cheese into the bowl of a food processor. Pulse until mixture is well combined. Spread in an even layer in a 9" x 13" baking dish.

Drain spinach by squeezing it in several layers of paper towels. Place spinach into the bowl of a food processor. Add water chestnuts, cream cheese, sour cream, mayonnaise, Parmesan cheese, roasted garlic, salt, lemon juice, and onion powder. Pulse until creamy and smooth. Pour into a disposable pastry bag and cut off tip of bag. Lay stencil on top of the artichoke dip. Use a sharp knife to trace around the outline of Frank's head. Remove stencil and pipe the spinach dip over the knife marks. Fill in Frank's head with spinach dip, so his entire head is green. Pour tortilla chips into a clean bowl in a food processor. Pulse to fine crumbs. Lay stencil over top of spinach dip. Sprinkle ground tortilla chips over cut out areas on stencil. Clean off excess crumbs using a pastry brush. Gently lift off stencil. Refrigerate for at least 30 minutes or up to 2 days. Serve cold.

*To roast garlic: Drizzle some olive oil over peeled garlic cloves. Loosely wrap in foil and roast in a 375 degree oven for 45 minutes.

CHEESY FRANKEN-HEADS

A simple Frankenstein shaped cookie cutter can transform store bought pie dough into little monsters.
Filled with gooey mozzarella cheese and decorated with green pesto skin, olive eyes, caper noses, and tomato mouths,
these adorable Franken-heads will be a hit with everyone at your party.

Ingredients:

1 package refrigerated pie crusts
Flour to dust counter top
1 egg
2 teaspoons water
8 slices mozzarella cheese
4 teaspoons prepared pesto
10 black olives, finely chopped
4 black olives, whole
8 capers, rinsed and patted dry
2 grape or cherry tomatoes

Special Equipment Needed:
    Frankenstein cookie cutter
    Rolling pin
    Plastic drinking straw
        or a #11 or #12 pastry tip

Cook's Notes:
You can create and decorate these
up to 2 days ahead of your party.
Cover and store in the refrigerator.
Bake just before your party begins.
They are best served hot.

Makes 8

Instructions:

Preheat oven to 425 degrees.

Thaw pie crusts according to package instructions. Unroll dough onto a lightly floured counter top. Use rolling pin to roll out dough to a 12" round. Cut out 16 Franken-heads using cookie cutter, re-rolling dough as needed.

Create egg wash by whisking egg and water together. Set 8 Franken-head dough pieces onto a parchment lined baking sheet. Brush egg wash over these Franken-head cut outs.

Cut slices of mozzarella cheese to fit within 1/4" of the sides of cut-outs (size will depend on the size of your cutter). Lay one cheese slice onto each of the 8 cut outs. Top with remaining dough cut outs. Seal edges by pressing both dough cut outs together all around edges.

Decorate Franken-heads.
Skin: Brush pesto all over top of dough cut outs.
Hair: Press chopped olives onto the top 1/2" of each head.
Eyes: Slice the outer edge off of the whole black olives to create a flat surface. Lay olive slice on cutting board. Use a straw or a large round pastry tip to cut round pieces out of the olives for eyes. Press onto dough.
Nose: Press one caper onto dough.
Mouth: Cut tomatoes into thin slices. Cut off a long strip of tomato. Place onto Franken-heads to create mouths.

Bake for 11-12 minutes. Serve hot.

CRISPY FRANKIE POPS

Rice crispy treats are metamorphosed into Frankenstein's monsters
by dipping them in green confectionery coating and decorating them with colorful modeling chocolate.
If you are looking for a great project for kids to do at your party, these are so fun to create and easy enough for even young kids
to decorate. Have the cereal treats dipped in the green coating before the party, and allow the kids to decorate.

Ingredients:

12 store bought rice cereal treats
16 oz. green colored confectionery
         coating wafers (candy melts)
1 recipe dark modeling chocolate*
Cocoa powder to dust counter top
1/2 recipe white modeling chocolate*
Red paste candy coloring
Green paste candy coloring

*Modeling Chocolate Recipe (Page 96)

To Color Modeling Chocolate:
Wear gloves! Pull off the amount of
modeling chocolate you would like
to color. Squeeze a few drops of
paste color onto the modeling chocolate
and knead until color is uniform. Add
more paste color until you reach the
desired shade. Make green and red.

Special Equipment Needed:
    12 wooden craft sticks
    Rolling pin
    Powder free latex or plastic gloves

Makes 12

12

Instructions:

Remove rice cereal treats from outer wrapper. Insert one craft stick into the bottom and up about 1 1/2" into a rice cereal treat. Repeat for all.

Pour green colored confectionery wafers into a microwave safe bowl. It is best to use a tall narrow bowl. Heat in microwave on high for 45 seconds. Remove and stir. Heat on high for 30 seconds. Stir. Heat on high for 20 seconds. Stir. If wafers are not completely melted, heat on high for 10 second intervals, stirring after each, until melted. (It is very easy to burn these wafers if you heat them for too long. If you do burn even a small amount, the entire batch is ruined. So, go slow!)

Hold a rice cereal treat by the craft stick and dip it into the green coating. Completely cover the rice cereal treat. Remove it from the coating, and let excess drip off. Lay it onto a parchment lined baking sheet (a size that will fit into your freezer.) Repeat. Place in freezer to harden the green coating, about 10 minutes. It is best to freeze pops within 2 minutes of dipping, so dip a few treats at a time and freeze. They will develop white streaks if they air dry for too long.

Dust counter top with some cocoa powder. Roll dark modeling chocolate out to 1/8" inch thickness. Cut 2" x 5" pieces, using a knife or pizza cutter. Cut along one long side to create hair. Brush off excess cocoa powder then press onto the top of each rice cereal pop. Cut off any excess modeling chocolate.

Create eyes using 2 small balls of white modeling chocolate and 2 very small balls of dark modeling chocolate. Create nose out of green colored modeling chocolate and mouth out of red colored modeling chocolate. Create bolts using dark modeling chocolate. Press decorations onto rice krispie pops, or use some green coating to "glue" decorations onto pops.

ABNORMAL BRAIN

Create this rich and creamy vanilla panna cotta brain in your own laboratory (kitchen)
using a brain shaped gelatin mold.
Your guests will gasp as they cut into the wiggly brain, but will smile with delight after just one bite.

Ingredients:

1 1/2 cups whole milk
2 tablespoons unflavored gelatin
1 cup granulated sugar
Pinch of salt
4 1/2 cups heavy whipping cream
4 teaspoons pure vanilla extract

Special Equipment Needed:
    Brain gelatin mold

Makes 1 (12-15 servings)

Instructions:

Pour cold milk into a large saucepan. Sprinkle the gelatin in a thin layer over the milk. Let stand for 10 minutes.

Heat the milk and gelatin mixture over high heat for 1 1/2 minutes. Stir constantly until the gelatin dissolves completely. Remove from heat. Stir in sugar and salt until dissolved. Pour cold heavy whipping cream and vanilla into pan and stir to combine.

Prepare an ice water bath in a bowl that is large enough to hold the saucepan. Cover the entire bottom of a bowl with ice cubes. Pour in enough cold water to cover the ice cubes. Set the saucepan into the ice water, being sure water does not flow into the pan. Stir the mixture frequently until it thickens slightly.

Set the brain mold into a towel lined bowl in order to keep it from falling over in the refrigerator. Pour chilled mixture into the brain shaped mold. Refrigerate at least 8 hours, or overnight.

To remove panna cotta brain from mold, fill your sink with hot water. Lower the mold into the hot water, so that the water comes up to the edge (but not over the edge.) Hold mold in hot water for 10 seconds. Remove and wipe water off bottom of mold. Place a plate (inverted) over opening of mold. Turn mold and plate over. Gently tug at the sides of the mold and the brain should release from the mold and drop onto your plate. Serve immediately, or return to the refrigerator for up to 5 days.

VAMPIRE and BAT CHIPS & BLOOD FONDUE

Fried flour tortilla chips shaped and decorated like bats and vampires are served up with blood red roasted pepper fondue.
Use a bat shaped cookie cutter to quickly create bat chips that taste so much better than tortilla chips out of a bag.
The Vampire Chips take a little more effort, but will surely impress your party guests (turn the page for Vampire Chip directions).

Fondue Ingredients:
2 -12 ounce jars roasted red peppers
1 small clove garlic, minced
2 tablespoons unsalted butter
2 tablespoons all purpose flour
1 1/2 cups whipping cream, warmed
8 ounces Gruyère cheese, shredded
8 ounces Havarti cheese, shredded
1 1/2 teaspoons red food coloring
3 drops green food coloring

Bat Chips Ingredients:
8 soft flour tortillas
Black paste color
6-8 cups vegetable oil for frying
Sea salt or table salt

Special Equipment Needed:
    Food processor
    Fondue pot
    Bat shaped cookie cutter
    Sponge brush roller
        (available at craft stores)
    Fryer or Dutch oven

Makes 30-50, depending
    on the size of your bat cutters

Fondue Instructions:

Drain and rinse roasted red peppers and pat dry with paper towels. Pour into the bowl of a food processor. Add garlic and puree until smooth, about 2 minutes.

Heat butter in a medium saucepan over medium heat until melted. Add flour and whisk constantly for 2 minutes. Pour warm cream into saucepan, whisking vigorously. Bring to a boil, stirring constantly. Continue to stir, and reduce heat to medium-low. Simmer until the sauce thickens, 2-3 minutes. Add a handful of cheese and continue to stir until cheese melts. Continue adding handfuls of cheese, stirring constantly, until cheese melts. Stir in food coloring and pour into a fondue pot. Keep fondue pot warm, but don't let fondue boil.

Bat Chips Instructions:

Use a bat shaped cookie cutter to cut bats out of tortillas. Pour a small amount of black paste color on a piece of tin foil. Roll a sponge brush roller over coloring until the sponge is completely black. Roll coloring over each bat shaped tortilla. Set tortillas in a single layer on a baking sheet.

Heat oil in a fryer or Dutch oven to 375 degrees. Fry bats, a few at a time, for about 1 minute until crispy. Remove from oil using a slotted spoon. Set on a paper towel to drain. Immediately sprinkle lightly with salt. Serve with Blood Fondue.

Cook's Notes: Store chips in an airtight container for up to a week. These chips will keep for up to 2 weeks if stored in a metal tin. If you don't have a sponge brush roller, you can use a pastry brush to color your Bat Chips. Just be aware that your brush may be stained pink after it is washed.

VAMPIRE CHIPS

Your guests will all want to know how you got an image of a vampire on your tasty tortilla chips.
The process, which is detailed below, is pretty simple but looks so amazing.
Your guests won't believe you made them yourself.

Ingredients:

10 flour tortillas (soft taco size)
1 can black food color spray*
Sea salt
6-8 cups vegetable oil

*Food color spray is available
  at cake decorating stores
  and craft stores.

Special Equipment Needed:
    Vampire Template (page 97)
    1 clear stencil sheet
    Hobby knife
    Kitchen shears
    Fryer or Dutch oven

Makes 40

Instructions:

To Create Vampire Stencil: Copy Vampire Template (page 97) onto copy paper. Set on a cutting board. Lay clear stencil sheet over image. Use your hobby knife to cut out all the black areas of the vampire image.

Cut each tortilla into 4 wedges. Lay a wedge on a piece of parchment paper. Set your vampire stencil over tortilla wedge. Hold food color spray over stencil, and lightly spray image (too much and the color will bleed). Remove stencil from tortilla. Pat stencil dry with paper towels. Repeat with remaining tortilla wedges. Wash stencil after about 10 uses and dry with paper towels.

Use kitchen shears to cut out the vampire shaped tortillas. Cut around the outer edges of the vampire image. Discard tortilla scraps or fry and enjoy as a snack.

Heat oil in a fryer or a Dutch oven to 375 degrees. Fry chips three to four at a time. Turn chips over after about 30 seconds and continue to fry for about 30 more seconds, until lightly golden brown and crispy. Remove chips from oil using a slotted spoon. Set on a paper towel to drain. Immediately sprinkle lightly with salt.

Allow to cool and serve with Blood Fondue.

Cook's Notes: Store chips in an airtight container for up to a week. These chips will keep for up to 2 weeks if stored in a metal tin.

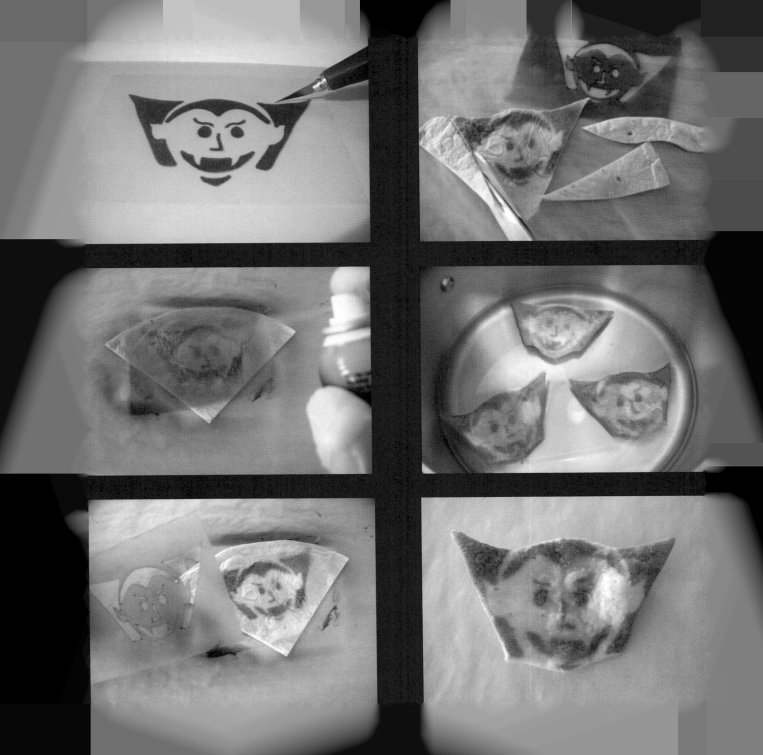

DREAMY DRACULA

As you sink your teeth into this Dreamy Dracula, ooey gooey, warm brie cheese will fill your happy mouth.
A sheet of puff pastry is wrapped around a wheel of brie and baked until golden brown.
It's decorated with black sesame seeds, olives, a tomato, and mozzarella cheese.

Ingredients:

1 sheet puff pastry
Flour for dusting counter top
1 (5"- 6") wheel of brie
1 egg
1 teaspoon water
2 tablespoons black sesame seeds
1 slice mozzarella cheese
2 jumbo black olives
1 small tomato

Special Equipment Needed:
    Small round cookie cutter (3/4")
    Pastry brush

*You may serve your Dracula on a platter.
For a more decorative look, cut a piece
of black paper into the collars of his cape
and set on a piece of red paper. Cover
the paper with plastic wrap or laminate
before adding the Dracula.

Makes 1 (8-10 servings)

Instructions:

Preheat oven to 425 degrees.

Defrost puff pastry according to package instructions. Dust counter top lightly with flour. Unfold thawed pastry onto floured surface. Smooth out any bumps and seal any cracks in dough. Lay wheel of brie into the center of the puff pastry. Wrap pastry dough around wheel of brie. Press seams together. Cut off any excess dough.

Whisk egg and water together. Brush egg wash over seams of dough. Lay seam side down on a baking sheet.

Create Dracula's hair by brushing egg wash over his head. Start the egg wash at one side of his head midway down the pastry. Brush up and around to the center of his face then brush down creating a point in the center of his head. Then brush from the point up and around to the other side of his head. Sprinkle black sesame seeds over the egg washed area.

Roll a small piece of the excess dough into a ball and press into the center of Dracula's face to create his nose. Brush egg wash over entire surface of dough.

Bake for 20-25 minutes until dough is puffed and golden brown. Let cool for 15 minutes. Move carefully to a serving platter.*

Use a small round cookie cutter to cut four circles of mozzarella cheese. Place two on the face for the eyes and two for the ears. Cut very small circles from the olives for the pupils and place them on top of the cheese eyes. Cut a strip of tomato for the mouth and place below the nose. Cut two fangs from the mozzarella cheese and attach to the underside of the mouth. Serve pastry warm.

BLACK BEAN BATS

If you are looking for a very quick recipe for your Halloween party, this one is great.
Spread homemade black bean dip onto a flour tortilla to create the black backdrop.
Cut a few bats out of another flour tortilla and place it on top. They are ready to go in the oven in minutes
and can be made ahead and kept refrigerated for up to 2 days.

Ingredients:

Black Bean Dip
15 ounce can black beans
2 tablespoons sour cream
2 tablespoons fresh cilantro leaves
1 teaspoon fresh lime juice
1/2 teaspoon cumin
3/4 teaspoon minced garlic
1-3 teaspoons finely chopped jalapeño*
Pinch salt and pepper, to taste

*add jalapeños according to your taste

6 flour tortillas (soft taco size)

Makes 3 (6-12 servings)

Special Equipment Needed:
    Food processor
    Bat shaped cookie cutter

Instructions:

Preheat oven to 350 degrees.

Rinse and drain black beans. Pour beans into the bowl of a food processor. Add sour cream, cilantro, lime juice, cumin, garlic, and jalapenos. Pulse until mixture is a smooth paste. Season with salt and pepper to taste.

Lay three tortillas onto baking sheets. Evenly divide black bean dip among tortillas. Spread over surface of each tortilla.

Cut two bats out of each of the remaining three tortillas. Place these tortillas over been dip covered tortillas and press gently to secure.

Bake for 8-10 minutes. Turn broiler on and broil for 30-45 seconds until tortillas become golden brown.

Serve hot or at room temperature.

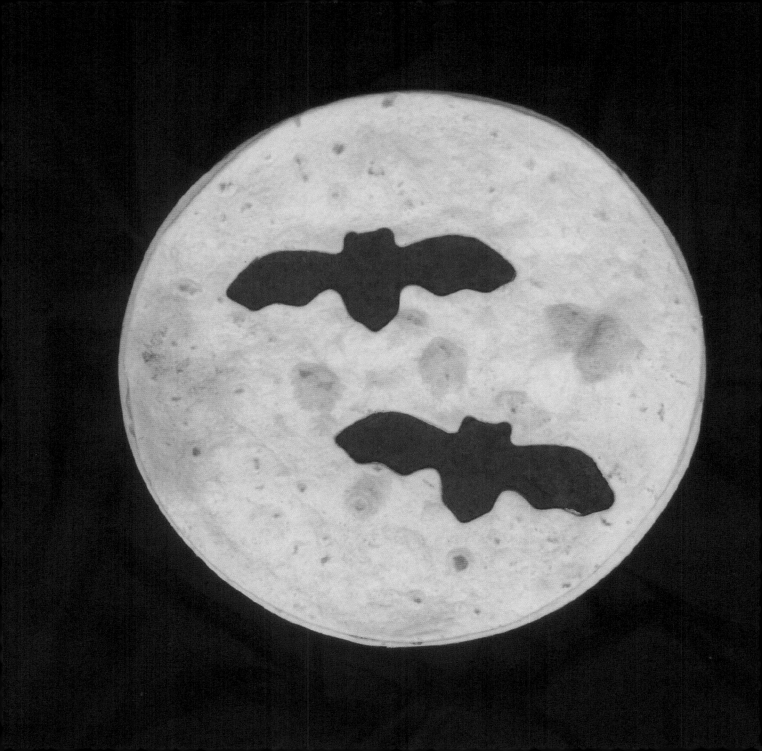

CHOCOLATE COFFINS

Rich and creamy chocolate ganache is dipped into dark confectionery coating to create these decadent coffin truffles.
Even if you have no candy making experience, you will be able to make this fun recipe.
You can purchase the confectionery coatings used to decorate these creepy coffins at cake decorating stores or craft stores.

Ingredients:

16 ounces semisweet chocolate
3/4 cup heavy whipping cream

16 ounces dark confectionery coating
4 ounces white confectionery coating

You can substitute semisweet and white chocolate for the confectionery coating if you are experienced in tempering chocolate.

Special Equipment Needed:
Coffin shaped cookie cutter
Pastry bag with coupler
#4 decorating tip

Makes 8-12
depending on size of coffin shaped cookie cutter

Create a double boiler. Set a saucepan filled with 1" of water over low heat. Set a bowl over the bottom saucepan, being sure the bottom of the bowl doesn't touch the water. Finely chop semisweet chocolate. Put in the top bowl of the double boiler. Add the heavy whipping cream. Stir often until the chocolate melts. Do not increase the heat.

Meanwhile, line an 8" square pan with non-stick aluminum foil, leaving some foil hanging over two opposite edges of the pan. Pour melted chocolate mixture (ganache) into the prepared pan. Place a piece of plastic wrap directly on top of mixture. Refrigerate for 2 hours.

Remove from refrigerator. Use the foil to lift ganache out of the pan. Cut ganache with coffin shaped cookie cutter. Use excess ganache for another use, or gently press together and cut with coffin shaped cutter.

Pour dark confectionery coating into a bowl. Heat on high in microwave for 30 seconds, then stir. Heat on high for 25 seconds, then stir. Heat on high for 20 seconds, then stir. If all the coating is not melted, continue to heat on high for 10 second intervals, stirring after each, until melted.

Set one ganache coffin on a fork. Dip it into the melted coating. Lift out of the coating and let excess drip off. Set on a parchment paper lined baking sheet. Repeat. Freeze coffins for 15 minutes.

Melt the white candy melts in the microwave (20 seconds, stir, 15 seconds, stir, 10 seconds, stir). Pour into a pastry bag fitted with decorating tip #4. Pipe border and cross decoration onto the chocolate coffins. Freeze for 5 minutes.

Bring to room temperature before serving. Store in an airtight container for up to 10 days.

MUMMY LASAGNA

Mozzarella eyes peer out from under noodle bandages in this cute mummy lasagna.
This is a great recipe to make for your kids on Beggars' Night.
Before your costume clad kids go out to beg for candy, give them a filling meal that will make them smile.

Ingredients:

2 cups marinara or spaghetti sauce
9 no-boil lasagna noodles
1 cup ricotta cheese
2 cups shredded mozzarella cheese
1/4 cup grated Parmesan cheese
1 egg
Pinch of salt
1 slice mozzarella cheese
Blue, red, and yellow food coloring

Special Equipment Needed:
    9" round baking dish or pie plate
    1 1/2" round cookie cutter
    3/4" round cookie cutter
    Small pastry brush

Makes 1 (4-6 servings)

Cook's Notes:
If you prefer, you can add the boiled noodle bandages and cheese eyes to the lasagna before baking, but the noodles will get a bit dry and the sauce will bleed through, turning the noodles red. Cover with non-stick foil and bake for 50 minutes.

Instructions:

Preheat oven to 375 degrees.

Spread 2/3 cup marinara sauce into the bottom of a 9" round baking dish. Top sauce with 3 sheets of lasagna noodles, broken into pieces to fit.

In a mixing bowl, combine ricotta cheese, shredded mozzarella cheese, Parmesan cheese, egg, and salt. Stir until mixture is creamy. Spread half of cheese mixture over layer of lasagna noodles. Top with 2/3 cup sauce, 3 more noodles then the remaining cheese mixture. Top with remaining sauce. Cover with tin foil and bake for 35 minutes.

Meanwhile, create noodle bandages. Bring a pot of water to a boil. Place remaining three lasagna noodles into boiling water and heat for 5-7 minutes until noodles are soft and pliable. Remove noodles from boiling water and set on a cutting board. Cut each noodle into 5 long strips. Set aside.

Cut two 1 1/2" circles and two 3/4" circles from the slice of mozzarella cheese. Squeeze one drop blue food coloring into a small bowl. Brush coloring over the 3/4" cheese circles. Add a drop of red coloring and a drop of yellow coloring to the blue coloring in the bowl. Stir to create black. Paint a black circle into the center of the blue colored cheese. Place one colored cheese circle on top of a 1 1/2" cheese circle, creating eyes.

Remove lasagna from oven. Place cheese eyes on lasagna and place strips of cooked noodles in a criss crossing pattern over lasagna to create the look of mummy bandages. Cover and return to oven for 15 minutes. Serve hot.

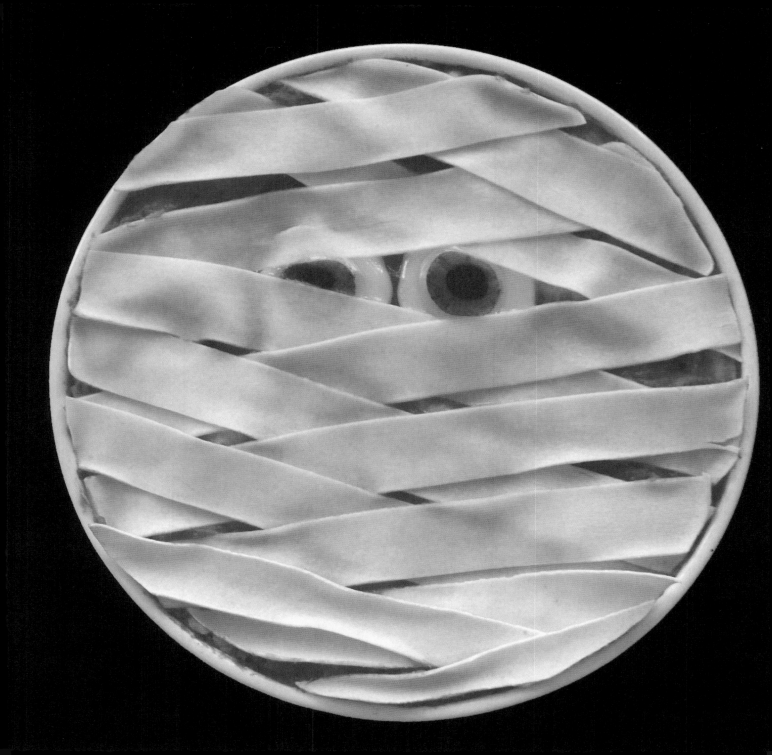

MUMMY SAYS "EAT YOUR VEGETABLES"

A simple veggie pizza decorated with strips of cream cheese is transformed into a mummy
that is so appealing, even your kids will eat their vegetables.

Ingredients:

1 tube crescent roll dough sheet
   (or one tube crescent rolls)
3 tablespoons Ranch dressing
1 1/2 cups chopped veggies
   (carrots, cucumbers, peppers,
   broccoli, tomatoes, etc.)
1 black olive
8 ounces cream cheese, softened

Special Equipment Needed:
   Mummy Head Template (page 98)
   White card stock paper
   Pastry bag
   #45 decorating tip

Cook's Notes: This veggie pizza can
be made up to 2 days ahead of
your party. Cover in plastic wrap
and keep refrigerated.

Instructions:

To Create Mummy Head Stencil: Copy Mummy Head Template (page 98),
increasing the size to fit an 8 1/2" x 11" page. Print onto a piece of card stock
paper. Cut out around the printed image. Discard the white part of the paper.

Preheat oven to 400 degrees. Line a baking sheet with parchment paper.

Unroll crescent dough, pinching together seams if necessary. Lay the stencil on the
dough. Cut around the stencil, discarding excess dough (or bake and enjoy). Set
dough mummy on baking sheet. Bake dough until golden brown, 8-12 minutes.
Let cool completely.

Spread Ranch dressing over cooled crust. Sprinkle vegetables evenly over crust.
Cut olive into slices. Place two equal size slices about 2"-3" from top of head for
eyes.

Fit a pastry bag with the decorating tip. Spoon cream cheese into the pastry bag.
Starting at the top of the mummy head, pipe strips of cream cheese across the
head, overlapping each to create bandages. Chill and serve cold.

CREEPY CREPE

Two white "chocolate" eyes peek out from underneath crepe bandages in this chocolate-hazelnut spread filled mummy. This is a sweet treat that will warm the hearts and tummies of your party guests.

Ingredients:

1/2 cup chocolate-hazelnut spread
12 store bought crepes
Black food coloring marker
8 white confectionery coating wafers

Special Equipment Needed:
   Pizza cutter

Makes 4

Instructions:

Preheat oven to 300 degrees.

Spread 2 tablespoons of the chocolate-hazelnut spread over one crepe.

To Create Eyes: Use a black food coloring marker to draw pupils on 2 white confectionery coating wafers. Press eyes onto chocolate-hazelnut spread covered crepe.

Cut 2 crepes into 1" wide strips using a pizza cutter or sharp knife. Layer strips in a criss cross pattern over chocolate-hazelnut spread covered crepe. Cut crepe into an 8" circle, cutting off excess. Use an 8" bowl turned upside down as a guide for a nice even circle.

Repeat to create a total of 4 Creepy Crepes.

Place crepes on baking sheets and heat in oven for 2-3 minutes, just until warm.

Serve warm.

Cook's Notes: Creepy crepes can be made in advance, covered in plastic wrap and refrigerated. Heat just before serving.

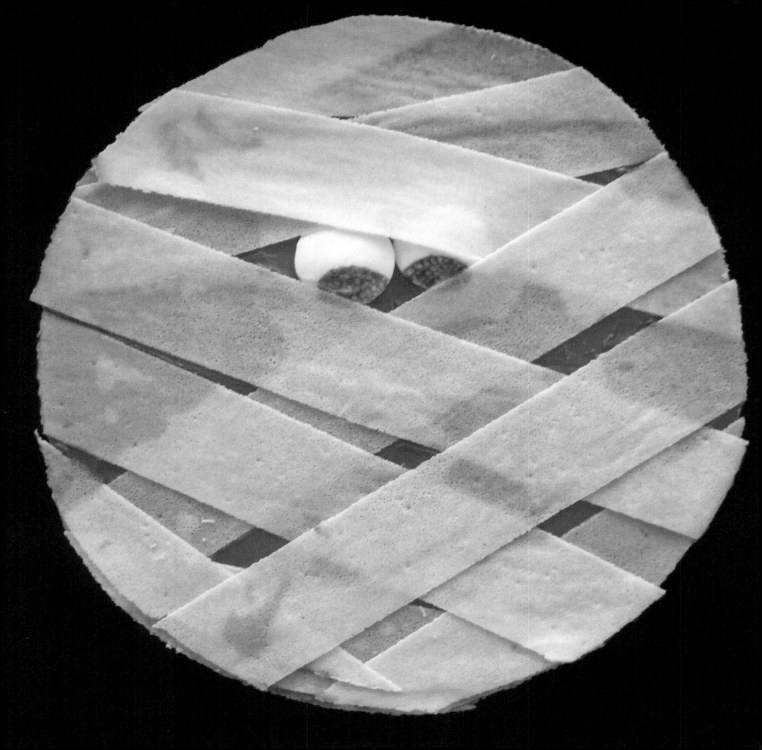

BLOODY MUMMY

Sweet red jam oozing out from under pie crust bandages makes this mummy come to life.
Store bought pie crust is cut into the shape of a mummy and is then covered with your favorite red jam.
Strips of pie crust are weaved across the mummy's body to create bandages that will bake up golden brown and crackling.
This mummy looks as if it just escaped from an ancient tomb.

Ingredients:

1 box refrigerated pie dough, thawed
    (2 pie crusts)
Flour to dust on work surface
3 tablespoons red jam
    (cherry, red raspberry, or strawberry)
1 egg, lightly beaten
2 chocolate chips
Flour for dusting counter

Special Equipment Needed:
    Mummy Template (page 97)
    White card stock paper
    Rolling pin
    Pastry brush

Makes 1 (4-6 servings)

Instructions:

To Create Mummy Stencil: Copy Mummy Template (page 97), increasing the size to 10" tall. Print onto card stock. Cut out image, discarding the white area.

Dust counter with flour. Unroll one thawed pie dough. Lay mummy stencil over pie dough. Use a knife to cut out dough around mummy stencil. Place pie dough mummy onto non-stick, foil lined baking sheet. Reserve dough scraps.

Unroll second pie dough onto counter. Use a rolling pin to roll out dough and dough scraps to thin them out slightly. Cut dough into strips about 1/4"-1/2" wide. Brush egg wash around the entire edge of the pie dough mummy. Use strips of dough to create a border around outer edge of the mummy. Press to secure border. Fill center of mummy with jam. Place chocolate chips in face for eyes.

Weave dough strips over mummy to create bandages. Press edges to secure and cut off excess dough. Brush mummy with egg wash. Freeze for 15 minutes.

Meanwhile, preheat oven to 450 degrees. Bake mummy for 12-15 minutes until crust is golden brown. Serve warm or at room temperature.

 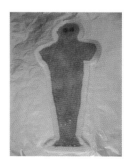   

WEREWOLF WON TONS

Won ton moons are imprinted with a silhouette of a werewolf. They are filled with spinach artichoke cream cheese and fried. Create a stencil from the template provided, and use black paste food coloring to paint a werewolf image onto won ton wrappers. Filled and fried these warm crunchy appetizers will have your guests howlin' at the moon.

Ingredients:

6-8 cups oil for frying
Black paste food coloring
32 round won ton wrappers
1 egg
1 teaspoon water
8 oz. spinach and artichoke cream
       cheese at room temperature

Special Equipment Needed:
    Werewolf Template (page 98)
    1 clear stencil sheet
    Hobby knife
    Sponge roller or sponge brush
    Pastry brush
    Disposable pastry bag or
        heavy duty zip top bag

To Create Werewolf Stencil:
Copy Werewolf Template (page 98) and print onto paper. Lay printed image on cutting board. Set clear stencil sheet over image. Use a hobby knife to cut out image of werewolf.

Makes 16

34

Heat oil in a fryer or a dutch oven to 375 degrees.

Pour out a small amount of black food coloring onto a piece of foil. Roll a sponge brush over coloring until sponge is completely black. Lay Werewolf Stencil over one won ton wrapper. Roll black coloring over the cut out areas of the stencil. Remove stencil and place won ton wrapper, image side down, onto a parchment lined baking sheet. Be sure not to move the printed won ton around once placed on parchment or the image will smear. Blot excess black paste coloring off of the stencil using a paper towel. Repeat to create a total of 16 printed won ton wrappers.

Lay the remaining 16 won ton wrappers on a parchment lined baking pan. In a small bowl, whisk egg and water together. Use a pastry brush to brush these won ton wrappers with the egg wash. Put cream cheese into a pastry bag. Cut off the tip. Pipe a tablespoon of cream cheese onto each of these won ton wrappers. Pick up one cheese topped wrapper and gently lay it, cheese side down, on top of the backside of a printed wrapper. Press edges together to seal. Repeat. Place won tons, image side down, into oil and fry until golden brown, about 1 minute. Serve hot.

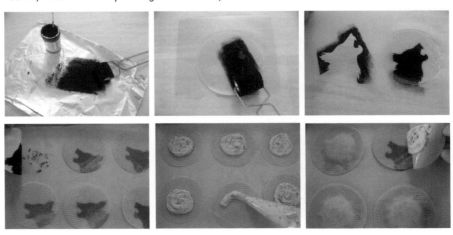

A store bought pizza crust is flavored with olive oil and garlic salt to create a the backdrop for this creature in the shadow of the moon.

Ingredients:

2 teaspoons extra virgin olive oil
1 (12") store bought pre-baked pizza crust
1/4 teaspoon garlic salt
12 ounces mozzarella cheese
1 (14 oz.) can jumbo black olives, drained

Special Equipment Needed:
        Howling Wolf Template (page 98)
        1 clear stencil sheet
        Hobby knife
        Baking stone or heavy duty
                        aluminum foil

Makes 1 (8-12 servings)

Instructions:

To Create Howling Wolf Stencil: Copy the Howling Wolf Template (page 98), increasing the size to fit onto an 8 1/2" x 11" page. Set the template on a cutting board. Set a clear stencil sheet over image. Use a hobby knife to cut out wolf image. Cut out eye and ear, keeping all cut out pieces.

Preheat oven to 450 degrees. Place a baking stone on the bottom rack (if you don't have a baking stone, put a double layer of heavy duty aluminum foil under pizza crust and bake directly on oven rack).

Brush olive oil over top of the pizza crust. Sprinkle garlic salt over oil. Sprinkle mozzarella cheese over entire pizza crust. Press down on cheese with your hands in order to compress the cheese into a more solid surface. Lay the stencil cut-out of the wolf over the cheese, aligning rounded bottom edge of the wolf with the edge of the crust.

Reserve one olive. Chop remaining olives into small pieces. Sprinkle chopped olives all around the wolf image onto the cheese topped pizza crust. Gently press olives onto cheese. Remove wolf stencil.

Cut reserved olive in half, lengthwise. Lay eye and ear stencil cut-outs over olive slices. Cut out a black olive eye and a black olive ear. Place eye and ear pieces onto the cheese wolf.

Reduce oven heat to 425 and place pizza directly onto the baking stone (or on tin foil directly on oven rack). Bake for 6-7 minutes until the cheese is melted. Broil for 30-60 seconds to crisp up the crust.

Serve hot.

WOLFIE POPS

These slightly scary looking werewolf lollipops are crafted from modeling chocolate
which tastes much like the very popular chewy chocolate candy rolls.
Dipped in chocolate coating and decorated with beady red eyes and fangs, these little pops are sure to scare up some fun.

Ingredients:

1 recipe dark modeling chocolate*
16 ounces dark confectionery coating*
  (or tempered semisweet chocolate)
1/4 recipe white modeling chocolate*
Red paste food coloring

*Recipes for modeling chocolate and
  directions for melting coating or
  chocolate are on page 96.

To Make Red Modeling Chocolate:
Put on your food handling gloves.
Pinch off about a tablespoon of white
modeling chocolate and add a few
drops of red paste food coloring.
Knead until chocolate is an even
color. Add more drops of red until
you get the desired shade of red.

Special Equipment Needed:
  12-15 lollipop sticks
  2 food handling gloves
  Toothpick

Makes 12-15

Instructions:

Pull off about 1 tablespoon of dark modeling chocolate. Roll it into a ball. Place
a lollipop stick into the ball. Pull off about a teaspoon of modeling chocolate and
roll into a ball. Press the smaller ball onto the front of the larger ball and smooth
it to form the werewolf's snout. Pinch off two small pieces of modeling chocolate
and mold them into ears. Affix the ears to the werewolf's head. Repeat with
remaining modeling chocolate, reserving about 2 tablespoons for the decorations.

Melt dark confectionery coating.* Pour into a tall narrow bowl or glass.

Hold one chocolate werewolf by the lollipop stick and dip into the chocolate
coating. Remove and let excess drip off. Allow to dry until the coating is tacky.
Use a fork to create the hair. Press the fork into the chocolate and pull away
quickly. This will form small hair like spikes in the coating (if the coating is too
warm, it will not form hair). Place Wolfie Pops in the freezer for 10 minutes.

To Decorate: Use remaining melted coating to adhere the features to the pops.

Eyes: Pinch off two small pieces of white modeling chocolate and roll into tiny
balls. Adhere to the wolfie's head to form eyes. Add two tiny balls of red and
two very tiny balls of dark modeling chocolate to finish the eyes.

Nose: Pinch off a small piece of dark modeling chocolate and roll it into a ball.
Elongate the ball and press a toothpick into it to create two nostrils. Adhere to
the tip of the wolfie's snout.

Fangs: Pinch off two small pieces of white modeling chocolate. Roll one piece into
a ball and continue to roll in between your fingers until a fang is formed. Attach
underneath the nose. Repeat.

WOLFMAN LOLLIES

Sink your fangs into one of these hand painted chocolate lollipops.
Painting chocolate lollipops is as easy as coloring in a coloring book, and the end result tastes so sweet.
This is a fantastic recipe to make with your kids.

Ingredients:

16 ounces milk confectionery coating
6 ounces white confectionery coating
   (or 2 oz. white, 2 oz. red, and
    2 oz. yellow wafers)
2 ounces dark confectionery coating
Yellow and red paste food coloring

*To Color White Confectionery Coating:
Add a few drops of yellow (or red)
paste food coloring to the melted
coating. Stir. Add more color if
necessary to reach the desired shade.

Special Equipment Needed:
   Electric skillet
   Wolfman lollipop candy molds
   16 lollipop sticks
   Food safe paint brushes
   Paste food coloring

Candy molds and supplies are
available on-line or at your local
craft or cake/candy decorating
supply stores.

Makes 16

Instructions:

Add about two inches of warm water to an electric skillet. Turn the heat setting to "warm" or the skillet's lowest setting.

Pour milk confectionery coating into a large glass cup. Pour dark coating into another cup. Pour 2 ounces of white coating into each of three cups, or fill one cup with white wafers, one with yellow wafers, and one with red wafers. Place into skillet, being sure that the water does not overflow into cups. Allow coatings to melt, stirring occasionally. Add coloring, if needed.*

To Decorate Lollipops: Use one paintbrush for each color of coating.

Dip a paintbrush into dark coating and dab it into the center of each of the eyes. Dab more dark coating into the noses. Dip a paintbrush into the red and paint the tongues. Place mold into freezer for 1-2 minutes. Remove mold and let come to room temperature, about 1 minute.

Dip a paintbrush into the yellow coating and paint directly over the dark coating in the eyes. Dip a paintbrush into the white coating and paint the fangs. Freeze for 1-2 minutes. Remove and let come to room temperature.

Spoon milk confectionery coating into the mold and fill the entire wolfman cavity. Place a lollipop stick into the stick cavity and press it into the coating. Spin the stick, being sure that the part that is in the lollipop is completely covered in coating. Freeze for 10-15 minutes. Remove mold from freezer and gently tug on stick. If lollipops come out easily, pull them out. If not, freeze for a few more minutes then remove. Let lollipops come to room temperature before serving.

This technique can be used to create vampires, mummies, monsters, and more.

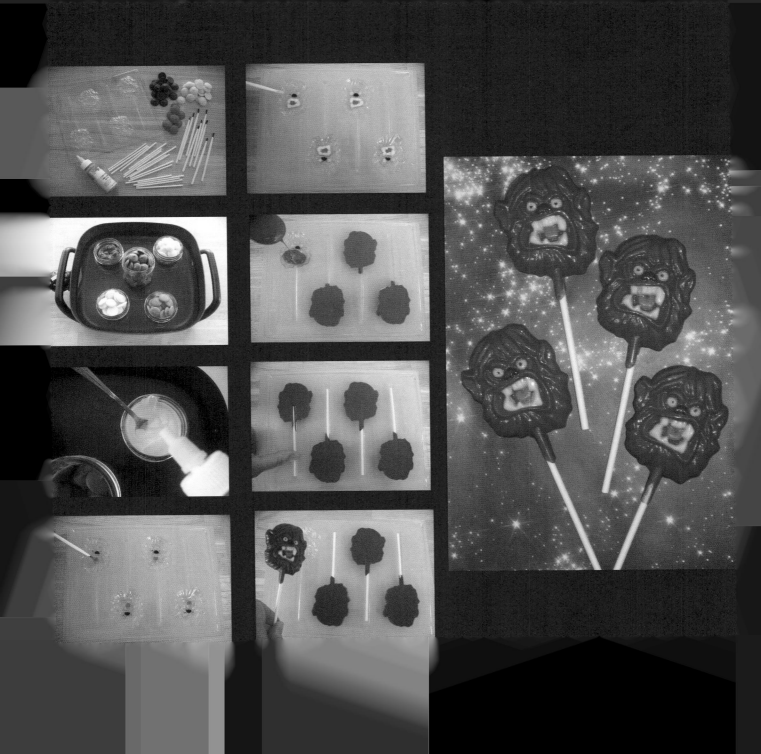

BEWITCHED BUFFET DÉCOR IDEAS

Decorate your home with items that would be found in a witch's lair. Fill an area with a store bought witch and surround her with black cats, rats, spell books, spiders, skulls, candles, and cauldrons.

Adorn shelves with unusually shaped bottles of potions' ingredients such as eye of newt and wing of bat. Add cobwebs and spiders to create the illusion that these sinister items have been around for many moons.

You can easily transform any room when you decorate your walls with plastic sheets that look like stone walls. These background scenes can be purchased at Halloween décor shops or on-line.

Display a store bought witch stirring a cauldron and add a black cat and broomstick to complete the scene. For an eerie effect, the night of your party add dry ice or a mister to the cauldron.

BEWITCHED BUFFET

Who has not wished,
at least for a moment,
to have magical powers?
Oh, to have the abilities of a witch,
and be able to turn someone
into a toad.
It would be fun to have
the powers of a witch,
if only for a night,
on Halloween.

You may not be able
to cast a spell,
but you can conjure up
a great party.
Use a little kitchen magic
to create dishes
that will bewitch your guests.

Gather all the ingredients to
mix up a cauldron filled with
bubbling Eww Brew,
or create your own
Cheesy Cauldron.

Put a spell on your guests
by serving them
Toasted Toads and Toadstool Tapenade,
or Wickedly Spicy Witch Dip;
or charm them with a
Charmed Cat Cake.

CACKLING CRACKERS & FULL MOON DIP

Homemade witch shaped crackers are served with a delicious hot chicken dip.
If you've never made crackers, you will be surprised at how easy they are to make in your home kitchen.
You can be creative and cut your crackers into different shapes like cats, bats, or even owls.

Ingredients:

Cackling Crackers
1 1/2 cups all purpose flour
1 1/2 teaspoons baking powder
3/4 teaspoon kosher salt
1 stick unsalted butter, divided
1/3 cup whole milk
1/2 teaspoon black paste food coloring
1 tablespoon olive oil
Table salt

Full Moon Dip (Chicken Dip)
8 ounces cream cheese, softened
3/4 cup mayonnaise
1 1/2 teaspoons lemon juice
2 teaspoons Worcestershire sauce
1 (12 oz.) can chunk chicken breast

Special Equipment Needed:
    Witch Template (page 98)
    White card stock paper
    Witch shaped cookie cutters
    Hand held mixer
    9" round ramekin or pie plate

Makes 24-36 crackers depending on
        size of cookie cutters

Cackling Crackers:

To Create Witch Stencil: Copy the Witch Template (page 98) increasing the size to 8" wide. Print onto a piece of card stock paper. Cut out image of witch.

Pour flour, baking powder, and kosher salt into the bowl of a food processor. Pulse three times. Add 6 tablespoons butter and pulse 10 times. Add milk and black paste food coloring and pulse until mixture forms a ball. If dough looks dry, add up to a tablespoon of milk.

Pour dough out onto a lightly floured surface. Knead 10 times. Divide dough into three balls. Pour olive oil into a shallow bowl. Place dough balls into bowl and coat them in the oil. Cover with plastic wrap and let rest for 30 minutes.

Preheat oven to 400 degrees.

Lightly flour work surface. Roll dough out as thin as possible. Lay witch stencil on dough and cut out around witch. Cut remaining dough with witch shaped cookie cutters, re-rolling as needed. Place cut outs on a parchment paper lined baking sheet. Prick each cracker all over using a fork. Melt remaining 2 tablespoons of butter. Brush crackers with butter and sprinkle salt, to taste, over tops. Bake for 8-12 minutes until crackers are crisp.

Full Moon Dip (Chicken Dip):

Combine cream cheese, mayonnaise, lemon juice, Worcestershire sauce, and chicken in a large mixing bowl. Beat with an electric mixer until combined. Spread into an 9" round ramekin or pie plate. Bake, covered with foil, in a 350 degree oven for 20 minutes. Top with large witch cracker and serve hot with remaining Cackling Crackers.

WICKEDLY SPICY WITCH DIP

A layered Mexican dip is adorned with a drawing of a witch that is created using black bean dip and guacamole.
You decide just how wickedly spicy you would like your witch.
Just add more or less jalapeño peppers to your recipe.

Ingredients:

1 pound ground sirloin (or ground beef)
1 packet taco seasoning
1/2 cup water
16 ounces refried beans
1 1/4 cups finely diced tomatoes
1/2 cup chopped black olives
1/4-3/4 cup diced jalapeños
3 cups Monterey jack cheese
1 cup sour cream
1 recipe black bean dip*
1 cup prepared guacamole
1 long slice Monterey jack cheese
4 strips of roasted red pepper
1 black olive

*Black Bean Dip ingredients list and
    preparation instructions on page 22

Special Equipment Needed:
    9" x 13" baking dish
    2 disposable pastry bags or
        heavy duty zip top bags

Makes 1 (Serves 12-18)

Instructions:

Preheat oven to 350 degrees.

Heat a large skillet over medium high heat. Add ground sirloin and cook until browned. Drain off fat. Add taco seasoning and water and bring to a boil. Lower heat and simmer until most of the liquid evaporates, 3-5 minutes.

Spread refried beans in the bottom of a 9" x 13" baking dish. Spread taco seasoned beef over beans. Sprinkle on tomatoes and olives. Decide how spicy you'd like the dip, and add jalapeños accordingly. Top with cheese. Cover with tin foil. Bake for 20-25 minutes until heated through and cheese is melted.

Remove from oven and let cool for 5 minutes. Remove tin foil. Spread sour cream in an even layer over top of cheese.

Spoon the black bean dip into a pastry bag. Cut off the tip off the bag. Use the picture of the Witch Dip on the opposite page as a guide (or create your own simple witch design). Pipe the black bean dip over the sour cream to create the outline of the witch, her hat, and her eye. Fill in the hat with bean dip.

Spoon guacamole into a pastry bag. Cut off the tip of the bag. Fill in the area of the witch's face with the guacamole, leaving the eye white. Pipe black bean dip over the green guacamole to create her hair, mouth, and eyebrow.

Add the slice of Monterey jack cheese to the witch's hat to form a band. Cut the roasted red pepper strips to form a buckle and set on the cheese band. Slice off the tip of the black olive and add it to the witch's eye.

Reheat dip for 5-10 minutes and serve hot with nacho chips.

46

HADDIE HINKLEBOTTOM'S HAT

Imagine cutting into this witch's hat and realizing that it is a huge peanut butter cup.
Peanut butter fudge is molded into the shape of a witch's hat and is coated in a rich and creamy chocolate glaze.
White modeling chocolate is used to create a hat band and buckle.

Ingredients:

Peanut Butter Fudge Hat:
11 ounces white baking chips
6 ounces peanut butter baking chips
1 1/4 cups creamy peanut butter
Pinch of salt

Chocolate Ganache Glaze:
8 ounces semisweet chocolate
1/2 cup heavy whipping cream
2 tablespoons light corn syrup

Decorations:
1/4 recipe white modeling chocolate
      (Recipe is on page 96)
Gold luster dust
      (A food safe gold dust used
      in cake decorating. You can find this
      at a craft or cake decorating store.)

Special Equipment Needed:
      5"-6" tall funnel
      6" round cookie cutter
          or a 6" round plastic lid
          that is about 1/2"-3/4" deep

Makes 1 (Serves 8-12)

Instructions: Pour white baking chips and peanut butter baking chips into a medium microwave safe bowl. Heat on high for 35 seconds. Remove from microwave and stir. Heat for 30 seconds, stir. Heat for 10 second intervals, stirring after each, until chips are all melted. Stir in creamy peanut butter and salt until smooth.

Line the funnel with plastic wrap. Set funnel into a bowl big enough to hold it upright. Pour peanut butter mixture into funnel. Freeze for 30-45 minutes. Lay 6" round cookie cutter on a parchment lined pan (or line a 6" round lid with plastic wrap). Reserve about 2 tablespoons of peanut butter mixture for later use. Pour remaining mixture into cookie cutter or lid. Freeze for 20-30 minutes. Remove items from freezer. Un-mold. Use some of the reserved peanut butter mixture to create the point of the witch's hat. The mixture should be fairly thick by this point. Just spoon some out and mold it with your hands into a cone shape and press it onto the top of the peanut butter hat. Reheat the remaining mixture for 3-5 seconds in the microwave. Use it to glue the two hat pieces together.

Finely chop semisweet chocolate and put into a medium sized shallow bowl. Heat heavy whipping cream and corn syrup in a small pot over medium high heat. Let mixture just come to a boil. Pour over chopped chocolate. Let sit for 3 minutes. Stir until creamy. Let sit until just slightly thickened, about 3-5 minutes.

Set peanut butter fudge hat on a tall glass set on a piece of parchment paper. Pour chocolate glaze over hat until entire hat is covered. Roll out white modeling chocolate and cut into a 1" band that is long enough to go around your hat. Wrap around hat and cut off excess. Cut a square out of modeling chocolate and create a buckle. Brush one side of buckle with gold luster dust. Brush some water onto the back of the buckle and attach it to the hat band. Set hat aside for at least two hours before serving so glaze stiffens and peanut butter fudge softens.

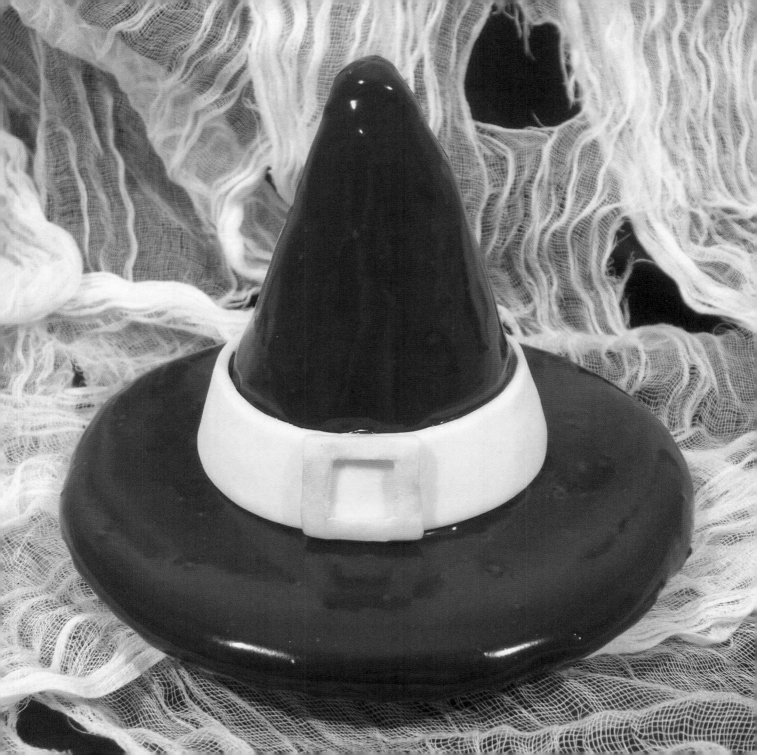

BEEFY BROOMSTICK

Hot dogs are wrapped in crescent dough and are transformed into a witch's broom in this unique version of pigs in a blanket.
What party would be complete without this all time favorite dish?
Surprise your guests with this clever version of a party classic.

Ingredients:

1 tube crescent seamless dough
   sheet (or crescent rolls)
4 beef hot dogs
1 egg
1 teaspoon water
4 drops red food coloring
4 drops green food coloring

Special Equipment Needed:
   Rolling pin
   Pastry brush

Makes 1 (Serves 6-10)

tin foil

50

Instructions:

Unroll tube of crescent roll dough. If using crescent rolls, pinch together all the seams. Use a rolling pin to roll sheet out to 9"x13 1/2".

Create broom handle. Cut one tip off of two hot dogs. Put cut sides together. Lay at one end of crescent dough sheet (along the short side). Roll dough over hot dogs to completely cover. Cut dough along edge. Seal edges together. Press dough around ends of hot dogs and seal. Round off ends. Whisk together egg and water. Brush some egg wash over the seams. Lay broom handle vertically in the center of a parchment lined baking sheet with seam side down.

Create broom bristles and band. Cut and reserve a 1" x 3" band of dough. Cut each of the remaining hot dogs vertically into four long pieces. Wrap as many hot dog pieces in dough as you are able (depending on the thickness of your hot dogs, you may have excess hot dog pieces). Seal all the seams and ends. Brush seams with egg wash.

Create the broom by attaching four bristles, laying seam side down, at one end of the broom handle. Fan these bristles out, leaving room in between each for additional bristles. Roll up some pieces of tin foil and place in between each of the four bristles. Set three bristles, seam side down, on top of the foil and attach to the handle. If you have more bristles, attach them to the outer edges of the broom. Place the dough band around the top of the broom bristles.

Brush egg wash over entire broom. Combine the red and green food coloring. Brush over the broom handle.

Bake for 25-30 minutes until golden brown. Remove foil. Use two spatulas to pick up broom and place on serving platter. Serve hot.

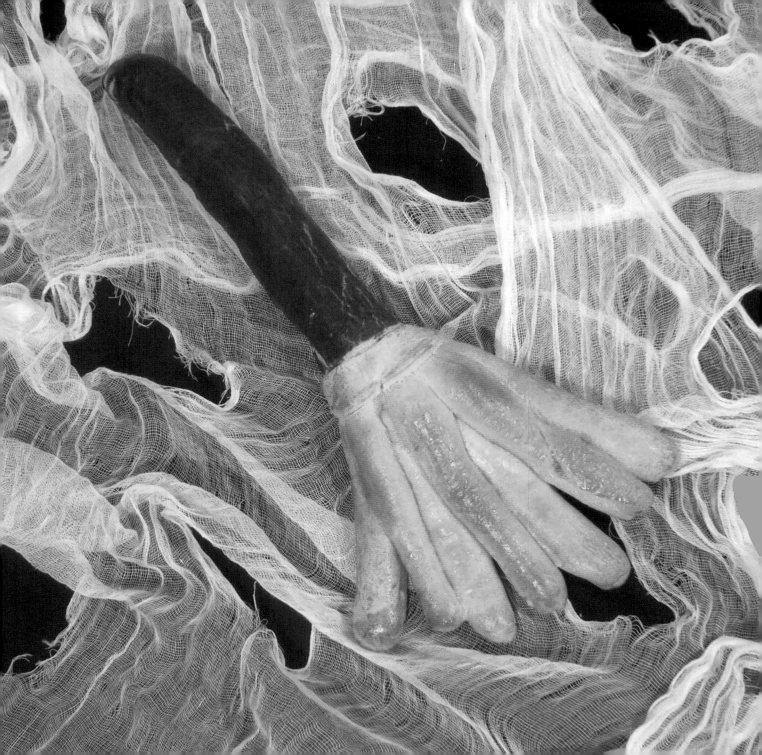

CHARMED CAT CAKE

Creamy vanilla frosting is stirred into crumbled up chocolate cake to create a rich and creamy "cake."
The mixture is molded into a cat head which is then covered in decadent chocolate ganache fur.
Modeling chocolate is colored and shaped into ears, eyes, nose, and whiskers to adorn this wickedly cute black cat.

Ingredients:

1 chocolate cake mix (egg, water, & oil)
1 (12 oz.) tub whipped vanilla frosting
8 ounces semisweet chocolate
1/2 cup heavy whipping cream
1/4 recipe dark modeling chocolate*
1/4 recipe white modeling chocolate*
Pink and green paste food coloring
*Modeling Chocolate Recipe (Page 96)
        Coloring Instructions (Page 12)

Special Equipment Needed:
    2 quart round bowl
    Cardboard cake round
    2 lollipop sticks

Makes 1 (Serves 8-12)

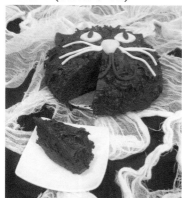

52

Instructions:

Prepare and bake cake according to package instructions. Let cake cool completely. Crumble cake into a large mixing bowl. Add vanilla frosting and stir until well combined. Line a round 2 quart bowl with a double layer of plastic wrap. Pour cake mixture into bowl. Cover with plastic wrap and press down to compact cake. Refrigerate for 1 hour.

Remove cake from refrigerator and remove top piece of plastic wrap. Cut a cardboard cake round to fit the opening of the bowl. Lay the cake round on the cake and invert the bowl. Remove bowl and plastic wrap.

Make chocolate ganache. Finely chop the semisweet chocolate and place in a shallow bowl. Heat whipping cream in a saucepan over medium heat, until it just begins to boil. Pour over chopped chocolate and let sit for 3 minutes. Stir until smooth. Let mixture sit until it thickens a little, 10-15 minutes, then spread over cake. To create hair, press a spatula onto the frosted cake and pull away quickly. The frosting should stand up in a point. Continue over entire cake.

To Decorate: Ear: Pinch off about 2 tablespoons of dark modeling chocolate and form it into a triangle. Press a lollipop stick into the base of the triangle about 1". Press stick into cake, leaving triangle ear exposed. Repeat for second ear.

Eyes: Pinch off 1 tablespoon of white modeling chocolate. Color with green food coloring. Shape into eyes and press onto cake. Add small dark pupils.

Nose/ Whiskers/Mouth: Color 1/2 tablespoon white modeling chocolate pink. Shape into a triangle and smooth edges for nose. Pinch off small pieces of white and roll it into very thin 4" long ropes, to create 6 whiskers. Do the same with some dark and create the mouth. Lay whiskers and mouth on cake. Add nose.

CHEESY CAULDRON

What witch party would be complete without a cauldron filled with bubbling brew?
Turn a simple cheese ball into a cauldron by embellishing it with a cream cheese brim and poppy seed stones.
Create a fire under the cauldron using bell pepper flames and pretzel rod logs.
Top it all off by adding bright green guacamole witch's brew.

Ingredients:

5 pretzel rods
8 ounces cream cheese, softened
4 ounces sharp cheddar cheese, shredded
1/2 cup real bacon bits
    (or crumbled bacon)
1/2 cup poppy seeds
1 yellow bell pepper
1 orange bell pepper
1/4 cup prepared guacamole

Special Equipment Needed:
    Food processor
    2 pastry bags
        or heavy duty zip top bags

Makes 1 (Serves 12-18)

Instructions:

Break off 2" pieces from each end of the pretzel rods. Eat or discard the center pieces. Spoon about 1 teaspoon of cream cheese into the center of a plate. Press the pretzels into the cream cheese, arranging them to look like logs on a fire.

Reserve 2 tablespoons of the cream cheese. Pour remaining cream cheese and cheddar cheese into the bowl of a food processor. Pulse until mixture is smooth and creamy. Add bacon and pulse just to combine.

Lay a large piece of plastic wrap on the counter. Spoon cream cheese mixture into the center of the plastic wrap. Use the plastic wrap to form the mixture into a ball.

Pour poppy seeds into a medium bowl. Roll cheese ball in the poppy seeds, leaving one end of cheese ball white. Place reserved cream cheese into a pastry bag. Snip off end. Pipe a ribbon of cream cheese around the edge of the white area on the cheese ball, creating the rim of the cauldron. Sprinkle poppy seeds over all the white areas of the cheese ball. Set cauldron onto pretzel logs.

Cut peppers into flames. Adhere them to the cauldron using any remaining cream cheese, or a dab of guacamole.

Spoon guacamole into a pastry bag. Cut off the tip and pipe guacamole into the top of the cauldron.

Serve with your favorite crackers.

Cook's Notes: Can be made up to 4 days before your party. Keep refrigerated.

BLACK WIDOW BITES

The thought of eating a spider is horrifying to most people, but they will have no problem wolfing down these black widows. Their furry little bodies are a soft and creamy combination of cookies and cream cheese with a crunchy cookie coating. Spindly little chocolate legs and red hot eyes make these little guys really come to life.

Ingredients:

18 ounces vanilla cream filled
    chocolate cookies
8 ounces cream cheese
6 ounces dark confectionery coating
    (or tempered semisweet chocolate)
60 red cinnamon candies

Special Equipment Needed:
    Food processor
    Disposable pastry bag
      or zip top bag

Makes 30

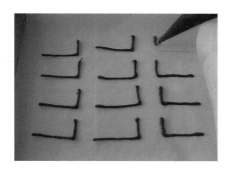

Instructions:

To Create Spider Body: Pour vanilla cream filled chocolate cookies into the bowl of a food processor. Pulse until cookies are finely ground. Remove 2/3 cup of cookie crumbs and place in a shallow bowl. Add cream cheese to food processor and pulse until mixture is well combined.

Scoop 30 heaping tablespoons of cookie mixture onto a parchment lined baking sheet. Roll one scoop into a ball and roll around in the cookie crumbs until it is completely coated. Repeat.

To Create Spider Legs: Melt confectionery coating according to directions on page 96. Pour melted chocolate into a pastry bag. Pipe out 8 "L" shaped spider legs for each spider body onto a parchment lined baking sheet (pipe extra as several of them will break as you assemble the spiders). Freeze to harden for 3-4 minutes.

To Create Black Widow Bites: Lay one cookie ball on the counter. Press 4 legs into each side of the spider body. Press 2 red cinnamon candy eyes onto spider. Repeat for all. Carefully pick up spiders and arrange them on a serving platter.

Cook's Notes: The bodies of these Black Widow Bites can be made up to three days before your party. Keep in an airtight container in the refrigerator. The day of your party, attach the legs and eyes and allow to come to room temperature before serving.

TOASTED TOADS & TOADSTOOL TAPENADE

Toasted wheat bread cut into toad shapes makes a great accompaniment to the tangy flavor of roasted mushroom and olive tapenade. This is a great do ahead recipe, so you don't have to fuss the day of your party.

Ingredients:

Toasted Toads:

1 loaf wheat bread
Olive oil spray
3 tablespoons grated Parmesan cheese
Salt

Toadstool Tapenade:

10 oz. Cremini mushrooms (toadstools)
3 large garlic cloves, minced
1 tablespoon olive oil
1/2 cup green olives with pimentos
2 roasted red peppers
1 tablespoon red wine vinegar
1 tablespoon finely chopped basil
1/2 teaspoon kosher salt
Pinch of black pepper
1/4 cup freshly grated Parmesan cheese

Special Equipment Needed:
    Toad shaped cookie cutter
    Food processor

Makes approximately 24 Toasted Toads

Instructions:

Toasted Toads:

Preheat oven to 350 degrees.

Cut slices of wheat bread with toad shaped cookie cutter. Discard scraps or make croutons. Spray both sides of toad shaped bread with olive oil spray. Lay in a single layer on a baking sheet. Sprinkle Parmesan cheese evenly over toads. Sprinkle lightly with salt, to taste. Bake for 15 minutes. Turn over toads. Bake for 10-15 minutes until crisp. Set aside to cool completely.

Toadstool Tapenade:

Place toadstools in a shallow baking dish. Add garlic. Drizzle olive oil over toadstools and garlic and toss to coat. Roast in oven for 30 minutes (you can roast the toadstools at the same time the toads are toasting). Remove from oven and let cool for 10 minutes.

Reserve 3 toadstools for garnish. Place remaining toadstools and garlic in the bowl of a food processor. Add the olives, roasted red peppers, red wine vinegar, basil, kosher salt, pepper, and Parmesan cheese. Pulse until mixture is chopped but still chunky. Pour into a serving bowl. Garnish with reserved toadstools.

Place bowl of toadstool tapenade onto a platter. Arrange toasted toads around bowl and serve cold.

Cook's Notes: Toasted Toads can be made ahead of your party and stored in an airtight container. Make and refrigerate toadstool tapenade up to 3 days ahead.

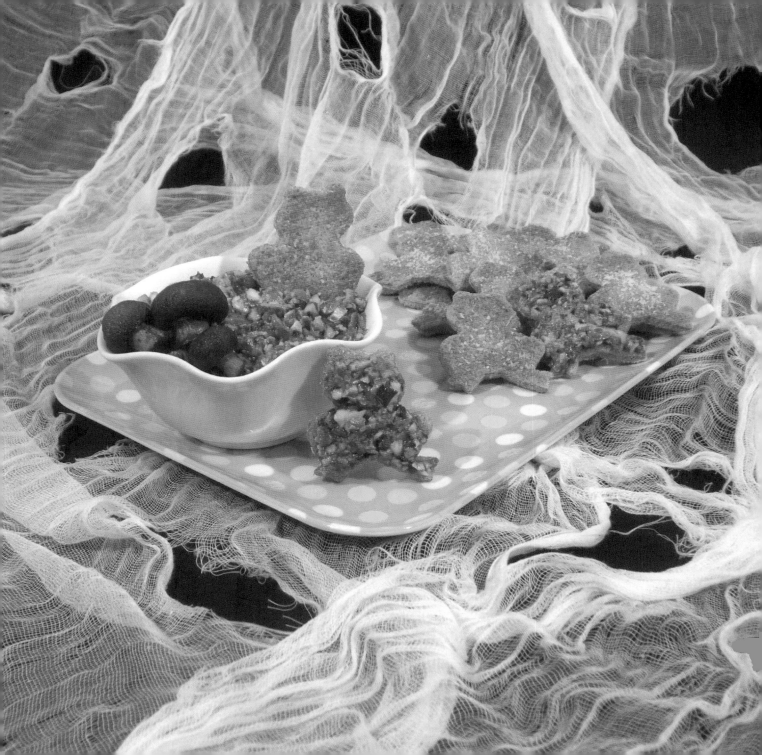

DIRTY BROWN RAT

This sweet rat is easily sculpted out of marshmallow cereal treats and adorned with a long tail made out of pink modeling chocolate. This is one rat you won't mind finding in your kitchen.

Ingredients:

Rat Body:
1/4 cup unsalted butter
10.5 ounces marshmallows
1 tablespoon cocoa powder
15 ounces cocoa crispy rice cereal

Rat Features:
1/4 recipe white modeling chocolate*
Pink paste food coloring
1/8th recipe dark modeling chocolate*
2 red candy coated chocolate candies

*Modeling Chocolate Recipe (page 96)

To Make Pink Modeling Chocolate:
Put food handling gloves on before you begin. Put one drop of pink coloring on the modeling chocolate. Knead until the color is even throughout.

Special Equipment Needed:
    Food handling gloves

Makes 1 (Serves 8-12)

Instructions:

Rat Body:
Heat butter, marshmallows, and cocoa powder in a large pan over low heat until melted. Pour cereal into a large bowl. Pour melted marshmallow mixture over cereal and stir until well coated. Let mixture cool until it is easy to handle, about 10-15 minutes.

Mold all of cereal into a big fat log. Round out the back end. Press the other end into a smaller curved point. Make an indentation about 3 inches from the point, to create the division between the head and the body. Smooth out any bumps and compress cereal until rat feels solid and you like its shape.

Rat Features:
Pinch off about 2 teaspoons of pink modeling chocolate. Roll into a 10" rope that is thicker at one end than the other. Use the back of a knife to make indentations all along the rope so it looks like a real rat's tail. Attach the tail by pressing it onto the back end of the rat.

Pinch off about 1/2 teaspoon of pink modeling chocolate and mold it into a triangle. Soften the edges and press it onto the front of the rat for the nose.

Pinch off about 1/2 teaspoon of dark modeling chocolate and mold it into a triangle. Pinch off a smaller piece of pink and make a smaller triangle. Press the two together to create an ear. Repeat. Press ears onto the top of the rat's head.

Pinch off a tiny piece of dark modeling chocolate and add it to the red candy to create eyes. Repeat. Press onto rat's face. Set rat on a serving platter.

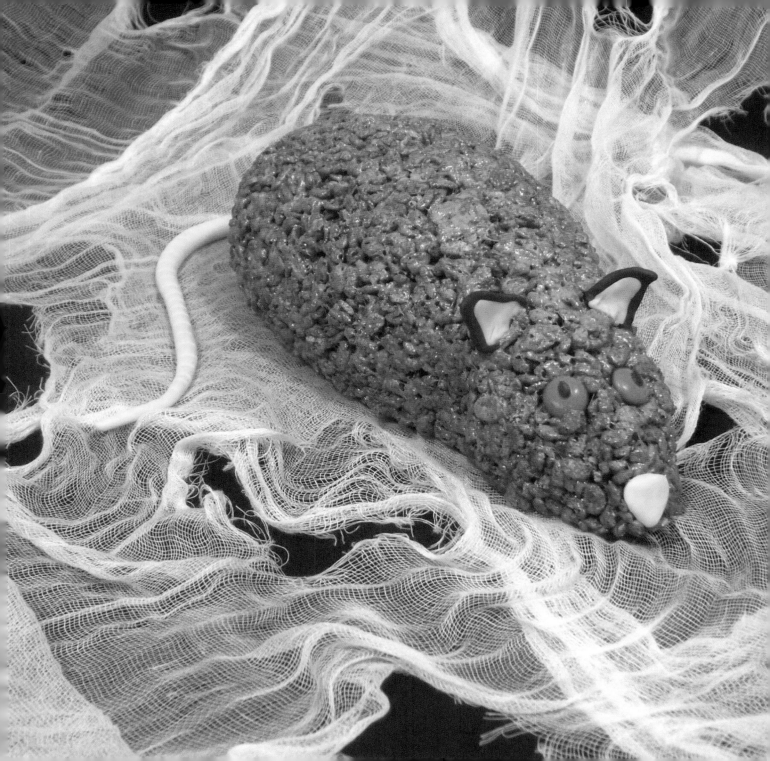

Eww BREW

A cauldron filled with bubbling popcorn is adorned with edible rats, bats, and frogs.
Neon green colored, white chocolate covered popcorn creates the bubbles in this creepy cauldron.
The creepy critters and body parts are hand painted and molded out of confectionery coating.

Ingredients:

White Chocolate Covered Popcorn:
1/2 cup popcorn kernels
12 ounces white confectionery coating
Neon green paste food coloring

Frogs, Bats, Fingers, Rats etc.:
White, dark, milk confectionery coating
Paste food colors

Special Equipment Needed:
    Air popcorn popper
    Plastic cauldron
    Assorted candy molds
        (rat, frog, bat, spider, heart,
        finger and/ or eyeball)

Makes 1 batch white chocolate
        popcorn (Serves 6-8)

Instructions:

White Chocolate Popcorn:

Pop popcorn in an air popper.

Place white confectionery coating in a microwave safe bowl. Heat for 25 seconds on high. Remove and stir. Heat for 20 seconds. Stir. Heat for 10 second increments, stirring after each, until coating is melted. Add a few drops of neon green food coloring and stir. Add more drops until you get the desired color.

Pour popcorn into a large bowl, removing any un-popped kernels. Pour melted coating over popcorn and stir just until popcorn is well coated. Spread on a parchment paper lined baking sheet. Refrigerate for 10-15 minutes. Remove from refrigerator and break up into smaller pieces. Fill the plastic cauldron with popcorn. You will need to make several batches of popcorn to fill a medium or large cauldron.

Frogs/Bats/Fingers/Rats etc.:

Follow instructions on page 40 for hand painting chocolates. Create any shapes that would go into a witch's brew. Add chocolate shapes to cauldron. If you don't have chocolate molds, you can also make Eww Brew ingredients by sculpting modeling chocolate into fun shapes; or simply purchase gummy frogs, spiders, rats, and body parts.

DEAD MAN'S DINER DECOR

Decorate your kitchen to look like a Fifties style diner filled with an abundance of gory details. Line your counter tops with severed body part props. Adorn your walls with homemade menu boards and diner signs. Hang bloody body part cardboard cutouts and fake blood stained gauze all over the kitchen walls and counters. Embellish with oversized plastic cleavers and knives.

For a real retro feel, attach opalescent silver paper or shiny tin foil to the sides of your counters and add diner stools.

Have your diner staff dress in classic waitress uniforms or aprons stained with fake blood.

DEAD MAN'S DINER

Halloween has become a time
when we seek out frightening experiences
and allow ourselves to step out
of our comfort zone.
Only on one night a year would we
even think to indulge in frightening fare.
Biting into a bloody severed hand
would be a ghastly experience
at any time of year,
but when that hand
is a hand shaped hamburger patty
served with ketchup on a bun
at a Halloween party,
eating a hand
becomes a fun experience.
Enjoy Bloody Finger Fries alongside your
Hand-Burgers and your
dining experience is elevated
to frighteningly good fun.
At your next Halloween party
surprise your guests with a menu filled
with Tina Melts, Stubbed Toe Subs,
Cannibal's Chowder, Toe Jam Sundaes,
and Feet Loaf.
Served hot to order,
the recipes in Dead Man's Diner
are sure to astound and delight
even the most squeamish of
Halloween party guests.

OPEN FACE SANDWICH

Imagine looking down at your meal and seeing a human face staring right up at you.
Mashed potatoes form an eerie face that sit atop a gravy covered turkey sandwich in this clever take on an open face sandwich.

Ingredients:

1 1/2 cups chicken stock
1/4 teaspoon salt
4 tablespoons unsalted butter
1/2 cup heavy whipping cream
1 1/2 cups potato flakes
Non-stick cooking spray
3 slices white bread
12 ounces deli sliced turkey
6 tablespoons turkey gravy, heated

Special Equipment Needed:
 5"-6" plastic face mold
  (either a candy, candle,
  or mask mold)

Makes 3

Instructions:

In a medium saucepan bring chicken stock, salt, and butter to a boil over high heat. Remove from heat and stir in heavy whipping cream. Add potato flakes. Stir with a fork until flakes are moistened.

Spray face mold liberally with non-stick cooking spray. Fill mold with mashed potatoes. Look at the underside of the mold to see if the mashed potatoes have filled up the nose cavity completely. If not, use the back of a wooden spoon to push the potatoes into the nose cavity. Set a piece of plastic wrap over potatoes and press down to compact potatoes. Set aside while you prepare a sandwich.

Lay a slice of bread on a dinner plate. Top with 4 ounces turkey. Spoon 2 tablespoons hot gravy over turkey. Remove plastic wrap from face mold. Invert mold over the sandwich and gently tug at the sides of the mold. The mashed potato face should slide out of the mold. If it doesn't, use a knife to separate the mashed potatoes from the mold in a few places. Invert again. Tug at the sides and allow mashed potato face to fall gently onto the sandwich. Serve immediately.

Spray the face mold with cooking spray before repeating process to create remaining two sandwiches.

Cook's Notes:
If you plan to make these for a large party, prepare the mashed potatoes just before your party begins. Pour a cup of chicken broth into the bottom of a crock pot then add the mashed potatoes. Keep the potatoes warm until the party begins. Stir the chicken broth into the potatoes just before making your first face. Keep the gravy hot in a small dip sized crock pot. It will be quick to assemble a sandwich when your guests place their order at the diner counter.

HAND-BURGER DRIPPING IN BLOOD

Biting into a severed hand would be a ghastly experience,
but when that bloody appendage is a hand shaped hamburger, eating a body part becomes a gas.
Use hand shaped cookie cutters to mold these little burgers. Cook and serve them on dinner rolls with dripping, blood red ketchup.

Ingredients:

1 slice white bread, crust removed
1 1/2 tablespoons milk
1/2 teaspoon salt
1/8 teaspoon ground black pepper
1 small clove garlic, minced
1 tablespoon ketchup
1 pound ground sirloin
Non-stick cooking spray
6 small dinner rolls, sliced in half
Ketchup

Special Equipment Needed:
    Hand shaped cookie cutter
    Indoor grill pan or skillet

Makes 6

Instructions:

Preheat oven to 275 degrees. Set a wire cooling rack on a baking sheet and spray with cooking spray.

Break bread into small pieces. Place in a mixing bowl. Pour milk over bread and mash with a fork until it forms a paste. Stir in salt, pepper, garlic, and ketchup. Add ground sirloin and stir, just to combine.

Spray a hand shaped cookie cutter with non-stick cooking spray. Press 1/6th of the mixture into the cookie cutter, being careful to press the meat into the finger area. Remove the cutter and use a spatula to transfer the Hand-Burger to the prepared rack. Repeat for remaining burgers. Bake for 12 minutes.

Spray an indoor grill pan (or skillet) with non-stick cooking spray. Heat over high heat. Remove Hand-Burgers from oven and place them onto grill pan. Sear on both sides. Cook to medium (140-145 degrees) or medium well (150-155 degrees). Serve on dinner rolls with ketchup.

Cook's Notes: Using ground sirloin will ensure that your Hand-Burgers remain in the shape of a hand when cooked. Fattier meats will lose their shape.

Baking the burgers before grilling them allows for even cooking of the fingers. You can cook the burgers to order at your party, or cook them ahead of time and keep them in a chafing dish. They will stay moist and delicious for hours in a covered chafing dish. Fill your chafing dish with a small amount of liquid (water or beef broth) before adding the Hand-Burgers. The steam will keep them from sticking and will help keep them moist.

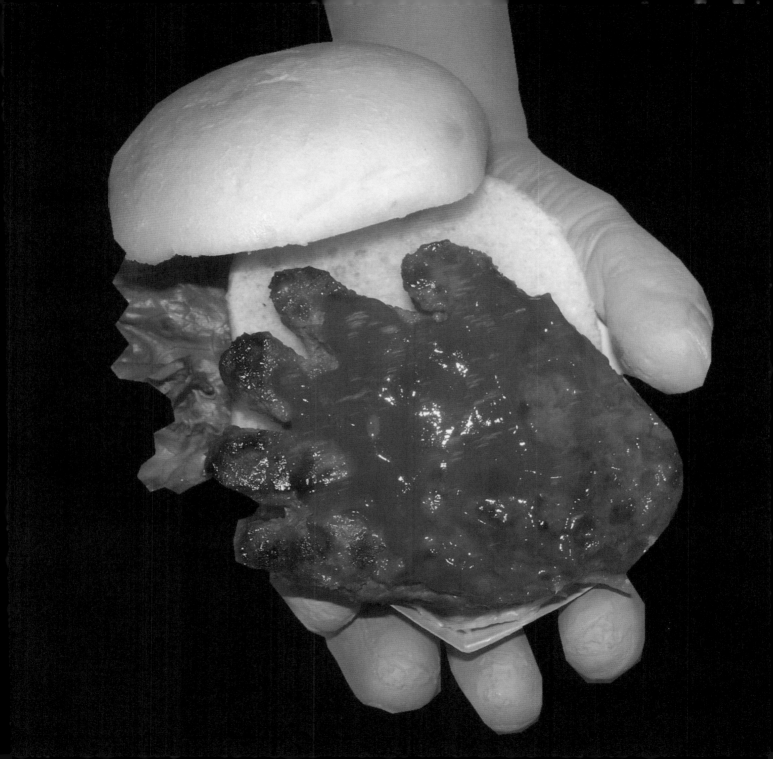

BLOODY FINGER FRIES

Severed fingers dripping in blood are the perfect accompaniment to a gruesome Hand-Burger.
These French fried fingers are created using a dough made from potato flakes.
Add creepy finger nails made from colored potato dough for a realistic effect.
Serve your crispy fingers dripping with blood red ketchup.

Ingredients:

6-8 cups vegetable oil for frying
1 1/3 cups potato flakes
1/2 teaspoon cornstarch
Pinch of salt, plus more for seasoning
2/3 cup water
1-2 drops red food coloring
Ketchup

Special Equipment Needed:
    Fryer or Dutch oven

Makes 36-40

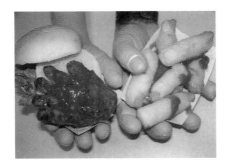

Instructions:

Heat oil in a fryer or Dutch oven to 375 degrees.

In a mixing bowl toss together potato flakes, corn starch, and a pinch of salt. Heat water in microwave for 1 minute. Pour over potato mixture and stir to combine. Use your hands to work mixture into a ball.

Pinch off about 1 teaspoon of dough and put in a small glass bowl. Add food coloring and mix until all dough is red. Set aside.

Pinch off about 1/2 tablespoon of dough and shape into a finger. Set onto a parchment paper lined baking sheet. Continue with all of the dough.

Put a small amount of water in a small bowl. Pinch off a small pea sized piece of the red dough. Hold the dough in between your index finger and thumb and flatten. Dab a bit of water onto one side of the dough and press onto the end of a potato finger. Be sure to press all around the fingernail. Repeat with all of the dough, attaching finger nails to all of the fingers.

Fry fingers for 2-3 minutes until they float and turn golden brown. Remove Finger Fries from oil using a slotted spoon. Set on a paper towel to drain. Immediately sprinkle with salt, to taste. Serve hot with ketchup.

Cook's Notes: You can fry all of your Finger Fries before your party. Place them on a baking sheet and cover tightly with foil. When ready to serve, heat them in a 350 degree oven for 8-12 minutes until crispy and hot.

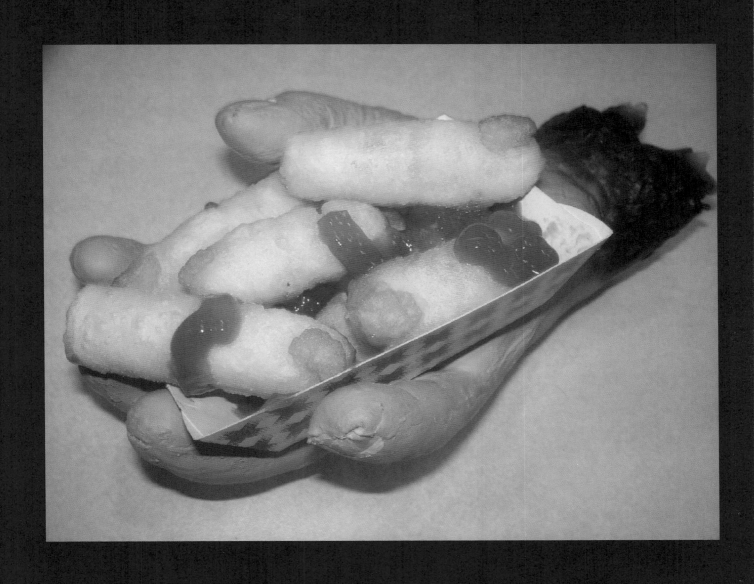

GRILLED FEET & BONE CHIPS

Little crusty feet filled with gooey melted cheese are served aside tiny, crispy bone chips.
Transform this classic diner fare into Halloween fun by simply cutting grilled cheese sandwiches with foot shaped cookie cutters.
Add homemade potato chips - slice potatoes and cut with a little bone shaped cutter and fry until golden brown.

Ingredients:

Grilled Feet:

12 slices white bread
6 American cheese slices
2 tablespoons butter, melted

Bone Chips:

6-8 cups vegetable oil for frying
6 russet potatoes, cleaned
Salt for seasoning

Special Equipment Needed:
    Foot and bone shaped
            cookie cutters
    Mandolin or very sharp knife

Instructions:

Heat a non-stick griddle over medium low heat.

Cut bread and cheese slices using a foot shaped cookie cutter (discard or eat scraps). Sandwich one cheese slice in between two bread slices. Spread butter on both sides of sandwich. Place on griddle and cook until both sides are golden brown and cheese is melted. Serve hot.

Heat oil in fryer to 350 degrees.

Cut potatoes into very thin slices using a mandolin or very sharp knife. Cut potato slices using a bone shaped cookie cutter. Discard excess potato (or fry and enjoy as a snack). Fry potatoes in small batches until golden brown. Drain on paper towels. Sprinkle immediately with salt, to taste.

Cook's Notes: Bone Chips can be made ahead of time and kept in an airtight container for up to a week. Get creative and add different seasonings to flavor your chips. Ranch dip mix, powdered cheese, or garlic salt are great options.

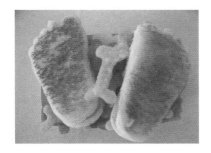  

STUBBED TOE SUB

Stubby meatball toes with grungy onion toe nails all smothered in blood red marinara sauce and gooey cheese peek out at your guests from in between a toasty sub bun.
This is one meatball sub your guests will not soon forget.

Ingredients:

3 garlic cloves, minced
1/4 cup ketchup
1 large egg, beaten
1/4 cup dried Italian bread crumbs
1/2 cup grated Parmesan cheese
1 teaspoon salt
1/4 teaspoon ground black pepper
1 pound ground chuck
1 large white onion
1 egg white, beaten
2 large sub buns
1 cup bottled marinara sauce
4 slices mozzarella cheese
4 slices provolone cheese

Special Equipment Needed:
   Kitchen shears

Makes 4 subs

Instructions:

Preheat oven to 350 degrees.

In a large mixing bowl stir together the garlic, ketchup, egg, bread crumbs, Parmesan cheese, salt, and pepper. Mix in the ground chuck. Scoop out about 2 tablespoons of the mixture and shape into a short stumpy log. Set on a non-stick foil lined baking sheet. Repeat with remaining mixture to create 28 toes.

Slice onion in half. Peel each layer, trying not to break onion. Cut onions into toenail shapes (about 3/4") using kitchen shears. Brush a small amount of egg white on tip of each meatball toe and press an onion toenail into each meatball.

Bake for 18-22 minutes until meatballs reach an internal temperature of 160 degrees. If any toenails fall off, dab a bit of ketchup on them to re-attach.

While toes are baking, cut sub buns in half lengthwise, then split each open and set on a baking sheet. Spread the marinara sauce evenly over the insides of the buns. Lay 1 slice mozzarella and 1 slice provolone on the top bun of each sandwich. Place in oven and bake for 6-10 minutes until cheese is melted and buns are golden brown.

Assemble sandwiches by placing 7 hot meatball toes on bottom buns. Make sure the toenails are facing out the front of each sandwich. Add top bun to sandwiches and serve hot.

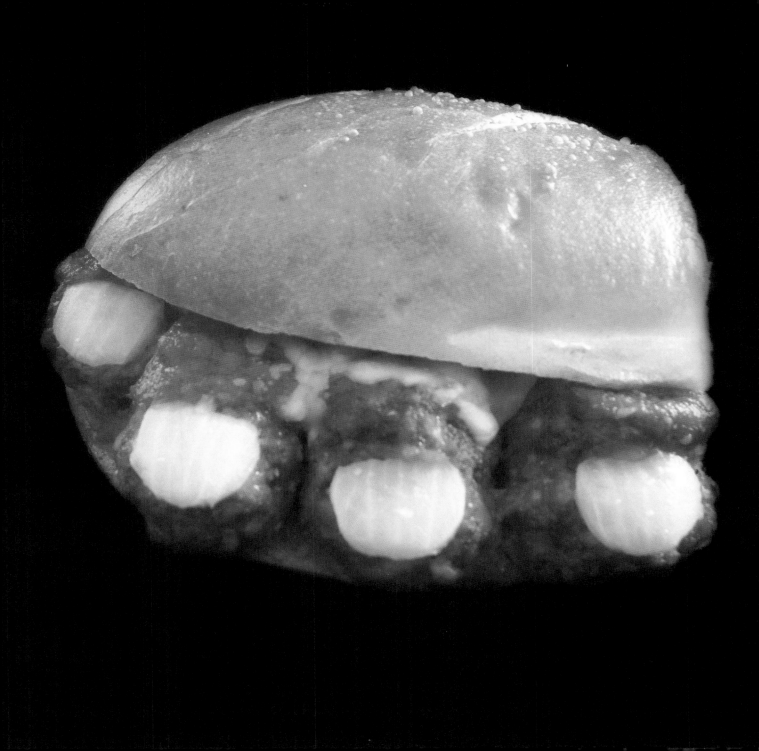

TINA MELT

Tuna melts are a favorite on diner menus around the country. Warm gooey cheese tops a toasted tuna salad sandwich. Your diner patrons will get a kick out of these little Tina Melt sandwiches cut into the shape of a ghostly girl.

Ingredients:

1 (5 oz.) can chunk light canned tuna
1/4 cup mayonnaise
1 tablespoons chopped onion
1 tablespoon chopped celery
10 slices white or wheat bread
5 slices American cheese
1 1/2 tablespoons butter, melted

Special Equipment Needed:
    Girl shaped cookie cutter

Makes 5 sandwiches

Instructions:

Drain tuna well.

In a mixing bowl, combine tuna, mayonnaise, onion, and celery. Mix well.

Cut bread and cheese slices using a girl shaped gingerbread cookie cutter. Discard scraps of bread and cheese (or make yourself mini cheese sandwiches for a snack).

Top each of the 5 bread slices with 1 slice of cheese.

Spread tuna mixture over cheese slices and top with remaining bread slices.

Spread butter on both sides of sandwiches.

Preheat non-stick griddle over medium heat. Cook sandwiches on both sides until golden brown and cheese is nicely melted. Serve hot.

Cook's Notes: Sandwiches can be assembled ahead of time and refrigerated until needed. Cook to order.

CANNIBAL'S CHOWDER

Warm chowder served up in a bread bowl is comfort food at its best.
Bake your bread in a skull shaped pan and embellish it with facial features,
and this bowl of comfort food gets a little scary.

Ingredients:

1 tube refrigerated French bread dough
Edible ink black food color marker
1 can clam chowder, heated
    (or your favorite recipe)

Special Equipment Needed:
    Non-stick skull shaped, mini cake pan

Makes 4

Instructions:

Preheat oven to 350 degrees.

Spray non-stick skull shaped, mini cake pan with cooking spray.

Open tube of bread dough. Cut into 4 equal pieces. Press each piece into a cavity in the skull shaped, mini cake pan.

Bake for 18-24 minutes until bread is golden brown.

Remove from oven and cool completely. Use the black edible ink marker to highlight the skulls' features. Draw in the eyes, noses and mouths.

Cut a circle out of the top of each skull then carefully hollow out bread, leaving a 1/4-in. shell (discard removed bread or save for another use).

Heat soup according to instructions on can. Fill each skull bread bowl with hot soup and serve to your guests.

Cook's Notes: Skull bowls can be made a day or two ahead of time and kept in an airtight container. Heat soup and fill bowls before serving.

FEET LOAF

Here's some good old fashioned meat loaf with a gory twist.
Sculpt this basic meat loaf recipe into two human sized feet and watch your guests squirm.
Once they take a bite, they'll come back for seconds.

Ingredients:

3 tablespoons finely minced shallots
2 large eggs, beaten
1 teaspoon salt
1/4 teaspoon black pepper
2 teaspoons Dijon mustard
2 teaspoons Worcestershire sauce
2/3 cup quick oats, finely ground
1/2 cup whole milk
2 lbs. ground meat loaf mix*
10 slices water chestnuts
1/4 cup ketchup

*Meat loaf mix is equal parts
 ground beef, pork, and veal

Special Equipment Needed:
    Non-stick aluminum foil
    Kitchen shears

Makes 2 Feet Loaves (serves 8-12)

Instructions:

Preheat oven to 350 degrees.

In a large mixing bowl, combine shallots, eggs, salt, pepper, mustard, Worcestershire sauce, ground oats, and milk. Gently stir in meat loaf mix. Divide mixture in two. Sculpt into a left and right foot and set each foot on a non-stick foil lined baking pan.

Using kitchen shears, cut water chestnuts into toenails and press onto meat loaf toes. To create the illusion of a severed foot, spoon 2 tablespoons ketchup on the foot where the leg would normally connect.

Bake for 45-55 minutes until meat loaves reach an internal temperature of 160 degrees. Remove from oven and let rest 15 minutes before slicing for your guests.

Cook's Notes: If you don't feel like you can hand sculpt two feet, purchase large food shaped chocolate molds (available on-line) to make easier work of this recipe.

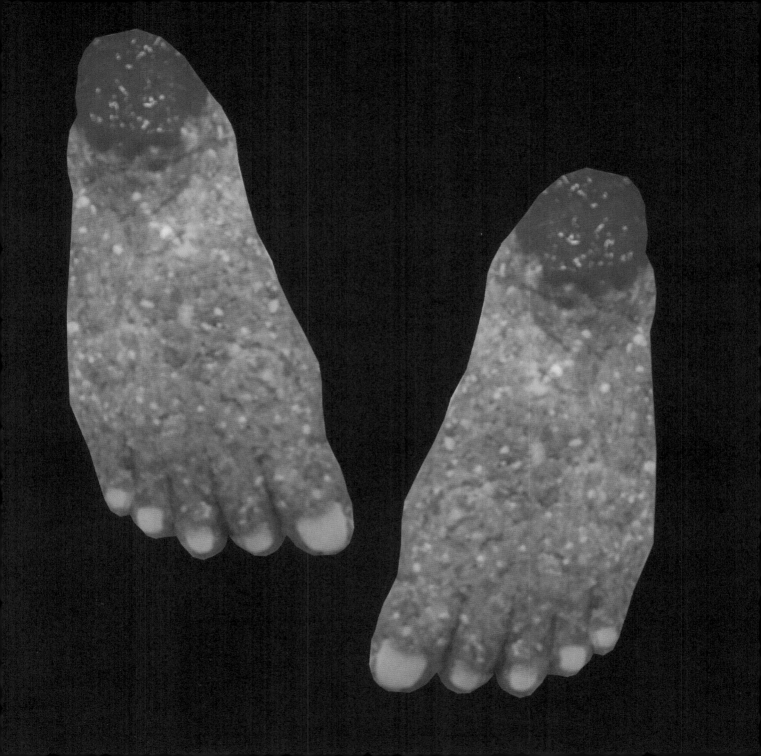

BONE CALZONES

Human sized bones are formed using pizza dough.
Fill these lifelike bones with bone marrow made from ricotta, mozzarella, and Parmesan cheese.
Serve with a side of blood red marinara sauce to make this a bone-chilling meal.

Ingredients:

1 cup ricotta cheese
4 ounces shredded mozzarella cheese
1 ounce grated Parmesan cheese
2 large eggs, divided
Pinch of salt
2 cans refrigerated thin crust pizza dough
1/2 cup marinara sauce

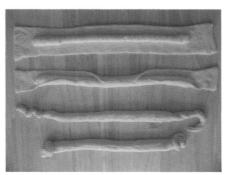

Instructions:

Preheat oven to 425 degrees.

Combine ricotta cheese, mozzarella cheese, Parmesan cheese, 1 egg, and salt in the bowl of a food processor. Pulse until smooth. Spoon mixture into a large pastry bag (or large zip top bag). Cut a hole in the tip of bag large enough to allow a 3/4" bead of cheese to flow out.

Open one can of pizza dough and lay out on counter. Press out to a 12" x 12" square. Cut into four 3" x 12" rectangles. Pipe cheese mixture down the center of each rectangle, leaving a 1 1/2" border at each end. Repeat with remaining dough and cheese. If you prefer shorter bones, cut each rectangle to 3" x 6".

Break remaining egg into a small bowl. Whisk in a teaspoon of water. Use a pastry brush to brush egg wash over all exposed dough. Bring one long side of dough up over the cheese. Bring the other long side of dough up over the cheese. Pinch together edges of dough to seal shut. Brush egg wash over seam.

Pull and twist the ends of each rectangle of dough, stretching the dough an additional inch or so. Tie each end into a knot.

Carefully pick up Bone Calzones and lay seam side down on a non-stick foil lined baking sheet. Bake for 9-11 minutes. Some cheese will ooze out of calzones during baking. Before transferring to a serving platter, cut off oozing cheese.

Heat marinara sauce and serve it alongside hot Bone Calzones.

Makes 8 long bones or 16 short bones.

GRAVE-Y STONES

A clever presentation of a traditional southern breakfast of hearty biscuits and gravy, these grave shaped biscuits are cut using cookie cutters and are engraved with a food color marker. As is tradition, they are served atop a creamy base of sausage gravy.

Ingredients:

1 cup all-purpose flour,
   plus more to dust the counter
1 teaspoon granulated sugar
1 teaspoon baking powder
1/4 teaspoon salt
3/4 cup heavy whipping cream
1 black food coloring marker
2 pouches store bought sausage gravy

Special Equipment Needed:
   Gravestone shaped cookie cutters

Makes 6-8, depending on size of cutters

Instructions:

Preheat oven to 450 degrees. Adjust an oven rack to the upper middle position.

Whisk together flour, sugar, baking powder, and salt in a mixing bowl. Pour cream over dry ingredients and stir just until mixture comes together.

Sprinkle some flour over your work surface. Pour dough onto work surface. Knead dough for 20-30 seconds until dough becomes smooth (don't over knead). Roll dough out to 3/4" thickness and cut with gravestone shaped cookie cutters. Place gravestones on a parchment paper lined baking sheet. Gently work together excess dough and cut with cookie cutters. Use black food coloring marker to write "R.I.P." on each gravestone.

Bake until golden brown, about 15 minutes, rotating baking sheet after 8 minutes.

Heat sausage gravy according to package instructions. Serve with warm gravestones.

Cook's Notes: You can use prepackaged biscuit dough to create your gravestones if desired. Purchase large sized biscuits and simply use gravestone cookie cutters to cut dough and bake per package instructions.

COTTAGE CHEESE BRAIN

Cottage cheese is a staple side dish on diner menus because it's nutritious brain food.
Transform this brain food into a "brain" simply by molding the cottage cheese into a brain shaped mold.

Ingredients:

15 ounces small curd cottage cheese
1 leaf lettuce for garnish
2 peach slices for garnish

Special Equipment Needed:
    Cheesecloth
    Strainer
    Plastic brain mold
        (available on-line)

Makes 2-4, depending on size of mold

Instructions:

Lay a double layer of cheesecloth in a fine mesh strainer, leaving some cloth hanging over the sides. Set the strainer over a large bowl. Pour cottage cheese into cheesecloth lined strainer. Take cloth that is hanging over the sides of the strainer and fold it over the cottage cheese. Refrigerate overnight to drain excess liquid from cottage cheese.

Remove cottage cheese from refrigerator. Press down firmly to release any remaining liquid. Remove from cheesecloth.

Press cottage cheese into brain mold. You may un-mold your cottage cheese brain immediately, but it will hold together better if you refrigerate it for at least one hour.

Garnish a plate with a piece of leaf lettuce. Invert mold and gently tug at the sides near the opening, allowing the cottage cheese brain to fall out. Garnish plate with peaches, if desired. Serve cold.

ONE-EYED JACK

An egg cooked inside a hole in a piece of toast is a childhood favorite of many diner patrons.
Transform this simple dish into something eye-catching by adding a pupil to the egg yolk
then pipe squiggles of ketchup around the egg white to resemble swollen blood vessels in a bloodshot eye.

Ingredients:

1 slice white bread
1 large egg
1 pat of butter
1 teaspoon ketchup
1 drop red food coloring
1 drop blue food coloring
1 drop yellow food coloring

Special Equipment Needed:
    3" round cookie cutter
    Small zip top bag
    Toothpick

Makes 1

Instructions:

Heat a 10" non-stick skillet over low heat for five minutes.

Meanwhile, use a 3" round cookie cutter to cut a hole in the center of one slice of bread. Toast bread until light golden brown.

Crack egg into a small bowl. Place butter in skillet and and let melt. Swirl to coat bottom of pan. Place toast in center of skillet. Gently pour egg into hole in toast. Cover skillet and let egg cook for about 3 minutes until the egg white is set and yolk is cooked to desired consistency (set or runny). Remove from skillet and place on a plate.

Pour ketchup into a small zip top bag. Cut a very small hole in one tip of the bag. Pipe squiggles around the egg white to resemble bloodshot eyes.

Stir together drops of red, blue, and yellow food coloring to create black. Dip a toothpick into the black coloring and prick a hole in the center of the egg yolk. This will create a small black dot. Carefully add more drops of black coloring to create a round pupil. Go slowly, adding very small drops one at a time, or the color will bleed.

Serve hot.

DEAD MAN'S FLOAT

What could be more eerie than a face appearing in your drink?
Transform the classic root beer float into a spooky diner drink by adding skull shaped vanilla ice cream.

Ingredients:

Vanilla ice cream
Root beer

Special Equipment Needed:
    Skull shaped ice or candy molds
      (silicone molds are best)
    Large zip top bag

Cook's Notes: This recipe does not provide specific amounts because you can fill your glasses with 4-12 ounces of root beer and use 1-4 scoops of ice cream. The float pictured on the next page was created in a small glass using 4 ounces of root beer, 1 scoop of ice cream, and 1 ice cream skull.

Let vanilla ice cream soften slightly.

Fill cavities of a skull mold with ice cream. Cover mold with plastic wrap. Fill a large zip top bag with ice cubes. Place mold in freezer. Lay bag of ice over mold and let ice cream skulls freeze overnight.

Remove ice cream skulls from molds by dipping the underside of the mold in hot water for 10 seconds, being sure to keep skulls dry. Turn mold over and tug at the sides of the mold. The skulls should pop out of the mold. If they don't, reheat them in hot water for a few more seconds and try again. Place skulls on a small sheet pan, cover tightly with plastic wrap, and freeze until ready to use.

To serve Dead Man's Floats: Scoop some ice cream into a clear glass. Place one or more ice cream skulls at the front of the glass. Fill glass with root beer. Serve immediately.

Suggestions for other diner drinks:

Chilling Cherry Cola
Squeeze red decorating gel along the rim of a glass, allowing it to drip down the sides.
Fill the glass with cherry cola and serve cold.

Moldy Malted
Add green food coloring to your favorite malted recipe for a gross, moldy looking drink.

Creepy Cocoa
Pour cocoa into a mug and top with a dollop of whipped cream. Add two mini chocolate chip eyes.

PEANUT BUTTER P-EYE

What diner meal would be complete without a piece of pie, or in this case, a piece of P-EYE.
This luscious peanut butter pie is made with creamy peanut butter and cream cheese.
To sweeten the pie, add vanilla and peanut butter baking chips. This combination creates an ultra rich and creamy filling.
Decorate with whipped cream, a chocolate cookie, and decorating gel to create the bloodshot eye.

Ingredients:

14 chocolate cream filled sandwich cookies
3 tablespoons butter, melted
1 1/2 cups vanilla baking chips (8 oz.)
3/4 cup peanut butter baking chips (4 oz.)
1 tablespoon unsalted butter
Pinch of salt
1 1/4 cups creamy peanut butter
8 ounces cream cheese, softened
8 ounces frozen whipped topping, thawed
3/4 cups heavy whipping cream, divided
3 tablespoons powdered sugar, divided
3/4 teaspoon pure vanilla extract, divided
20 drops blue food coloring
1 chocolate cream filled cookie
1 tube red decorating gel

Special Equipment Needed:
  9" pie plate
  Electric mixer and whisk
  4" round cookie cutter

Makes 1 (Serves 8)

Instructions:

Pour cookies into the bowl of a food processor. Pulse to fine crumbs. Pour in melted butter and pulse until mixture looks like wet sand. Press into the bottom and up the sides of a 9" pie plate. Set aside.

Combine vanilla baking chips, peanut butter baking chips, and butter in a microwave safe mixing bowl. Heat on high for 30 seconds. Stir. Heat for 20 seconds. Stir. Then heat for 10 second increments, stirring in between each, until melted. Stir in salt and peanut butter until smooth.

In a mixing bowl, beat cream cheese until fluffy. Beat in peanut butter mixture until fluffy. Beat in whipped topping. Spoon filling into crust. Smooth out filling in a rounded mound.

In a mixing bowl, combine ½ cup whipping cream with 2 tablespoons powdered sugar and ½ teaspoon vanilla. Whisk until stiff peaks form. Use to frost entire surface of pie. Combine remaining ¼ cup heavy whipping cream, 1 tablespoon powdered sugar, ¼ teaspoon vanilla extract, and 20 drops blue food coloring. Whisk until stiff peaks form. Set cookie cutter in the center of the pie. Spoon blue whipped cream into the cookie cutter. Smooth out, then remove cookie cutter. Smooth out blue whipped cream into a nice circle, creating an iris. Remove one half of cream filled sandwich cookie and clean any cream off cookie. Place cookie in the center of the pie, creating the pupil. Pipe squiggles of red decorating gel around the eye, creating the effect of a bloodshot eye.

Refrigerate for 1 hour or up to 4 days.

Cut pie into 8 slices and serve cold or at room temperature.

TOE JAM SUNDAE

Sounds gross, doesn't it?
But this dish is really de-lish.
Surround scoops of vanilla ice cream with banana toes adorned with almond toe nails, and top them off with caramel toe jam. Yum!

Ingredients:

5 scoops vanilla ice cream
2 mini bananas
5 slivered almonds
2 tablespoons caramel sauce

Makes 1

Instructions:

Scoop ice cream into a dessert cup.

Cut bananas into 1" pieces. Use the four end pieces to create toes. If using middle slices, carve into points using a small knife.

Press a slivered almond into the pointed end of each banana slice.

Arrange banana toes around ice cream scoops.

Drizzle Caramel Sauce over sundae. Serve immediately.

Optional Version:

3 large scoops vanilla ice cream
3 mini bananas
6 slivered almonds
1 tablespoon strawberry sauce
1 tablespoon pineapple sauce
1 tablespoon chocolate sauce
Whipped cream
Chopped nuts
1 maraschino cherry

Makes 1

Banana Split Version of Sundae:

Place three ice cream scoops down center of a banana split dish.

Create banana toes as above. Arrange around the outside of the ice cream scoops.

Spoon strawberry sauce over one scoop of ice cream. Spoon pineapple sauce over center scoop of ice cream. Spoon chocolate sauce over remaining scoop of ice cream. Top with whipped cream. Sprinkle chopped nuts over top of whipped cream and add the cherry.

MODELING CHOCOLATE
and chocolate melting methods

This recipe is used throughout the book to create decorations for sweet treats.
Make up a batch of white and dark modeling chocolate, wrap tightly in plastic wrap, and store in a zip top bag.
The modeling chocolate will keep for a few months if stored in a cool dry place.
To add vivid color, knead paste food coloring into modeling chocolate.
To keep your hands from turning color, be sure to wear food handling gloves when adding color.

White Modeling Chocolate:
16 ounces white chocolate
1/4 cup light corn syrup

Dark Modeling Chocolate:
16 ounces semisweet chocolate
1/2 cup light corn syrup

Confectionery coating can be used in place of pure chocolate. Confectionery coating is featured in recipes throughout this book because it is easy enough for even a novice to use. It is a chocolate product made with hydrogenated oils instead of cocoa butter and doesn't require tempering. This product is available in milk, dark, white, and even colored varieties. These coatings can be purchased from craft or cake decorating supply stores in wafers or blocks.

Special Equipment Needed:
  Digital read thermometer

Finely chop chocolate and melt in a double boiler or the microwave.

Double Boiler Method: Heat 1" of water over low heat in a saucepan. Place a bowl over the saucepan, being sure the bottom doesn't touch the water. Put chocolate in bowl and stir occasionally until melted.

Microwave Method: Pour 16 ounces chopped chocolate or confectionery coating wafers into a microwave safe bowl. Heat for 30 seconds. Stir. Heat for 20 seconds. Stir vigorously. Heat for 15 seconds. Stir vigorously. If not all melted, heat for 10 second intervals, stirring in between each until melted. Do not rush this process, as chocolate can burn easily. If you do burn the chocolate, throw it away and start over in a clean bowl.

To Create Modeling Chocolate: Let melted chocolate cool to 91 degrees, stirring often. Pour in corn syrup and stir until thickened. Pour out onto a counter top (preferably marble or granite) and knead until glossy and smooth. If you add the corn syrup when the chocolate is too hot, the cocoa butter or oil will rise to the surface and you will have a greasy mess. All is not lost as you can continue to knead the chocolate until all of the oil is absorbed back into the chocolate. This can take a while, but don't give up. Eventually it will become smooth and glossy. If you don't have a thermometer, test the temperature of the melted chocolate by putting a drop on your lip. It should feel cool. If it's hot, let it cool longer.

To Store Modeling Chocolate: Wrap tightly in plastic wrap and store in a zip top bag or airtight container. Keeps for months if stored properly.

Vampire (recipe page 18)

Templates

To find full size printable templates go to
http://www.HungryHalloween.com/

Cut stencils out of clear stencil sheets
which can be purchased at craft stores.

Monster (recipe page 8)

Mummy (recipe page 32)

Templates

To find full size
printable templates go to
http://www.HungryHalloween.com/

Witch (recipe page 44)

Werewolf (recipe page 34)

Mummy Head (recipe page 28)

Howling Wolf (recipe page 36)

PARTY PLANNING TIPS

Get organized. Keep a notebook filled with ideas, recipes, timetables, guest lists, and an R.S.V.P. checklist. I use a three-ringed binder filled with plastic page protectors so I can add magazine clippings and ideas printed from websites.

Give yourself plenty of time to decorate your house. It always takes longer than you think it will, especially if you are building sets and props, as we do each year. Halloween decorations are readily available in late summer at most party supply stores and discount stores, but the Halloween prop shops don't usually open until October 1st. Large props can be purchased from on-line resources, but I like to see the props up close to check their quality before buying. Also, don't forget to shop at dollar stores. You'd be surprised at the decorations you can find very inexpensively. I suggest you try to decide your party theme a year in advance so you can take advantage of the huge discounts offered at the end of the Halloween season. I tend to buy all of my expensive props for at least half off their regular prices.

Plan some fun activities, especially for your younger guests. Every year I host a separate kids' party, so I can focus all of my energy on entertaining the kids. They do fun craft projects, eat kid-friendly food, and play lots of exciting games. I give big prizes to the winners but always have small prizes for everyone so no one feels left out. I purchase most of my prizes at incredible discounts (up to 90% off) at the end of the Halloween season. For our teen parties we simply play music and show movies. I get the teenagers in my family involved by allowing them to host their own parties with my supervision. They have fun helping to decorate and planning their own menu. Our adult parties are all about great food and good friends, but we do hire a tarot reader to entertain our guests. If you would like specific party activity ideas, visit my website: **http://www.HungryHalloween.com/**.

Decide on the date, time, and length of your party. If you are planning a kids' party, host it on a weekend afternoon. Kids are active and alert during the day. Also, if you plan the party in between lunch and dinner, you will only need to serve snacks and drinks. Teenagers and younger adults prefer their parties to begin in the late evening on a Saturday and will party until well after midnight. These party guests will tend to eat the least, so plan accordingly. If you are hosting mostly older adults or families, I suggest starting your party around dinner time on Saturday. Your guests will come hungry and you can enjoy their company for several hours.

Select your menu. Choose to make a few of the elaborate recipes from this book as well as a few of the less complicated ones. Fill in with veggie trays, cheese, dips, and chips. I like to have a huge spread of food at my parties, but I can't make it all by myself, so I ask friends and family to help. If you are short on time or help, or your budget is tight, you may opt to try something I have done in the past. I asked my guests to bring a dish and I offered a prize for the guest who brought the best themed food item. My guests felt like they were an integral part of the party as everyone enjoyed and talked about their creativity.

Don't forget to have fun!

INDEX

ABOUT THE AUTHOR

Beth Jackson Klosterboer is passionate about Halloween and is excited to share her imaginative Halloween recipes, decorating ideas, and party planning tips with you. Beth and her husband Jim have hosted over a dozen Halloween parties for hundreds of guests and have spent countless hours creating recipes and decorations for each event. Beth has worked as a chocolatier and event planner for over 20 years and has owned and operated BJaiz Yum Yum Shoppe and Candy Garden retail candy stores. She loves to teach the art of chocolate making and has taught well over 1000 students. Since 2008, Beth has won numerous national and local recipe/cooking contests as well as several national essay contests. For more recipes and ideas from Beth, check out her website: **http://www.HungryHalloween.com/**.

Made in the USA
Charleston, SC
28 June 2010